Scrapbooking THE SCHOOL  YEARS

THE EDITORS OF MEMORY MAKERS BOOKS

M

Memory Makers Books
Cincinnati, Ohio

WWW.MEMORYMAKERSMAGAZINE.COM

Scrapbooking the School Years. Copyright © 2007 by Memory Makers Books.
Manufactured in the United States of America. All rights reserved. It is permissible
for the purchaser to make the projects contained herein and sell them at fairs, bazaars and
craft shows. No other part of this book may be reproduced in any form or by any electronic or
mechanical means including information storage and retrieval systems without permission in
writing from the publisher, except by a reviewer, who may quote a brief passage in review. Pub-
lished by Memory Makers Books, an imprint of F+W Publications, Inc., 4700 East Galbraith Road,
Cincinnati, Ohio 45236. (800) 289-0963. First edition.

11 10 09 08 07   5 4 3 2

Distributed in Canada by Fraser Direct
100 Armstrong Avenue
Georgetown, ON, Canada L7G 5S4
Tel: (905) 877-4411

Distributed in the U.K. and Europe by David & Charles
Brunel House, Newton Abbot, Devon, TQ12 4PU, England
Tel: (+44) 1626 323200, Fax: (+44) 1626 323319
E-mail: postmaster@davidandcharles.co.uk

Distributed in Australia by Capricorn Link
P.O. Box 704, S. Windsor, NSW 2756 Australia
Tel: (02) 4577-3555

Library of Congress Cataloging-in-Publication Data

Scrapbooking the school years / from the editors of Memory Makers Books.
     p. cm.
  Includes index.
 ISBN-13: 978-1-892127-99-0 (pbk.: alk. paper)
 ISBN-10: 1-892127-99-7 (pbk.: alk. paper)
 1. Photograph albums. 2. Photographs--Conservation and restoration. 3. Scrapbooks.
 4. School children--Collectibles. I. Memory Makers Books.
 TR501.S45 2006
 745.593--dc22
                              2006031079

EDITORS: KAREN DAVIS, AMY GLANDER
ART COORDINATOR: EILEEN ABER
DESIGNER: MARISSA BOWERS
LAYOUT ARTIST: NEAL MILES, RIGHTEOUS PLANET DESIGN, INC.
PHOTO STYLIST: NORA MARTINI
PHOTOGRAPHERS: ROBERT BEST, TIM GRONDIN, KRIS KANDLER,
AL PARRISH AND CHRISTINE POLOMSKY
PRODUCTION COORDINATOR: MATT WAGNER

CONTRIBUTING ARTISTS

JESSIE BALDWIN

AMBER BALEY

LISA DIXON

KATHY FESMIRE

KITTY FOSTER

JENNIFER GALLACHER

ANGIE HEAD

BARB HOGAN

VANESSA HUDSON

CAROLINE HUOT

KIM KESTI

SHARON LAAKKONEN

BRENDA MCANDREWS

KIM MORENO

KELLI NOTO

BARB PFEFFER

SUZY PLANTAMURA

HEATHER PRECKEL

KATHLEEN SUMMERS

CHRISTINE TRAVERSA

DENISE TUCKER

CONTENTS

INTRODUCTION   **6**

ABCs, 123s   **8**
[Preschool-Grade 1]

THE WHEELS ON THE BUS   **36**
[Grades 2 - 5]

HOMEWORK
TIME   study

You hate it. And so do I. The homework hour. Every single day. It's been a struggle ever since you started school, years ago. When you get home, you just want to relax, play and move. After dinner, you are much too impatient, tired and easily irritated. So the homework hour is right around 4 pm. You get all settled on the kitchen table with dictionary, calculator, agenda and books on hand. And most importantly, your eraser! for all the times you need to start over!

$ 4 PM

I know you've

SAVED BY THE BELL   64

[Grades 6 - 8]

GOING PLACES   92

[Grades 9 - 12]

STAR STUDENTS   120

[Contributing Artists]

SOURCE GUIDE   124

INDEX   126

Seth Thomas

When my daughter was in kindergarten, she created a special Mother's Day gift and proudly presented it to me along with a flower in a Styrofoam cup. My daughter's handprints embellish a poem that reminds mothers that although we sometimes "get discouraged" because we find "handprints on furniture and walls," our children are constantly growing and someday "all those tiny handprints will surely fade away." This construction paper masterpiece still hangs on the side of our refrigerator. And my kids know that if they can convince me to read the poem aloud, I will cry.

SCRAPBOOKING THE SCHOOL YEARS is about capturing the memories before those days are gone. It's so fresh at the moment and yet the memories fade so quickly. Kids really do grow up fast! One day you're dropping them off for the first day of preschool and before you can blink a teary eye, they're graduating from high school and heading off to college!

Without the photos, without the journaling, will you remember all of the little details? What did their kindergarten backpack look like? How nervous, or calm, were they when they sang their first solo or spoke their first part at the school concert? Can you name their first best friend? Were they happy or scared to switch classes in junior high? What is their favorite subject in high school?

Whether you and your children are beginning this journey through the school years or are reflecting back on the trip, *Scrapbooking the School Years* will inspire you to scrap the memories! Create pages about the big events (first day of school, field trips, prom, graduation) and the small details (back-to-school shopping, after-school routines, growth during the school year, favorite subjects).

Grab your camera and a journal; snap those photos and jot down those cute or profound things that your children say. We can't stop our children from growing up fast, but we can record the moments to laugh about and cherish in the years to come!

CHAPTER 1

ABCs, 123s

[Preschool - Grade 1]

Though you always knew this day would come all too fast, nothing could prepare your heartstrings for the moment your child turns to cling to your leg one last time before dashing off to explore a brave new world. These first years of school are perhaps hardest on parents, as we watch our children launch, all too gleefully from our comfort zones, into their first flights of independence: preschool, kindergarten and first grade. These school years make us catch our breath with the reality of how the wrinkly, bundle of joy we were just playing Pat-a-Cake with on our knee is now learning to read and write, while discovering the joys of painting and eating paste. It's the moment you've both been working toward since your child took his first steps. Scrapbook your child's preliminary pursuit of formal education to savor every year and all its wondrous changes, keeping these moments forever where they belong: in your heart and within sight.

OCCUPATION: FULL-TIME STUDENT

BARB PFEFFER
OMAHA, NEBRASKA

The monumental transition of climbing the classroom ladder to become a full-time first grader is taken in stride by Barb's daughter. Barb used simple, crisp lines, with strips of patterned paper and letter stickers, to play up the confidence and determination found in the photos. She added childhood whimsy and feminine fun with large, patterned paper circles and playful, flower stickers. A red and green complementary color scheme coordinates perfectly with the photos and elicits the feeling of well-grounded enthusiasm.

Supplies: Patterned paper, flower stickers, tags (KI Memories); letter stickers (SEI); rub-ons (Scrapworks); cardstock

MEMORABILIA CHECKLIST

* ★ Preschool or kindergarten graduation diploma, program, tassel
* ★ Concert or play program
* ★ School papers
* ★ Field trip brochures, maps, itinerary
* ★ Report cards
* ★ Bus number tag
* ★ School supplies list
* ★ Snack lists
* ★ Welcome letter, thank-you notes or other "happy" notes sent home from teacher
* ★ End-of-year activities schedule

The biggest change for you in starting school this year is going from being a half-day kindergartener to being a full-day first grader! It's a little daunting, but it's a challenge you seem ready to meet head-on. Your confidence amazes me. You are not the slightest bit nervous to start first grade. The look on your face says "bring it on!" I know you will excel in your new occupation as full-time student!

FIRST LUNCH BOX

JESSIE BALDWIN
LAS VEGAS, NEVADA

With first days of school come first lunch boxes, as Jessie's daughter, Violet, proudly displays on this milestone layout. Jessie enlarged the focal-point photo, which emphasizes the large, white letter stickers on the bottom of Violet's new accessory, and then mounted it at an angle on the page. Chipboard flowers and frames, sanded for texture, surround both photos for lighthearted charm and dimension, while square frames repeat the lunchbox shape throughout the layout for thematic effect.

Supplies: Cardstock; chipboard accents (Pressed Petals); rub-ons (Imagination Project); sandpaper; gel pen

DROP OFF PICK UP

SUZY PLANTAMURA
LAGUNA NIGUEL, CALIFORNIA

First-day-of-preschool jitters turned into joy for Chloe, as is evident in this celebratory layout of transformation. Suzy used black-and-white photos to capture the raw emotions of her daughter's first day, and set them against sherbet-sweet colors that focus on the ending high-note. Wavy borders, cut along the inner top and bottom patterned paper strips, express the roller coaster of emotions experienced, while black ink along the edges of the chipboard letters, set overtop the strips, add emphasis to the title blocks. Suzy stamped the flower accents, which she then cut out and enhanced with markers.

Supplies: Patterned paper (Autumn Leaves); flower stamps (Adorn It); chipboard letters (Li'l Davis Designs); ribbon, rickrack (source unknown); circle cutter; solvent ink; marker; pen; cardstock

LUNCH PAIL NOTES

SUZY PLANTAMURA
LAGUNA NIGUEL, CALIFORNIA

Suzy's daughter, Sophie, receives a special treat each day when she opens her lunch box to find lunch pail love notes from Mama. Using a girly mix of pretty pastels and sunny brights, Suzy trimmed various cardstocks into 3" x 5" (8cm x 13cm) note cards and embellished them with a garden of die-cut hearts and flowers constructed from foam. Multi-colored rhinestones add a charming twinkle, while ribbon and handwritten messages create a homespun touch.

Supplies: Cardstock; die-cut flowers and hearts (Ellison); large staples (EK Success); ribbons, rhinestones, foam (source unknown); pen

BACK TO SCHOOL DAY

CHRISTINE TRAVERSA
JOLIET, ILLINOIS

Christine's daughter took tiny, timid steps into her classroom, which led to the big step of becoming an official preschooler. Christine used photoediting software to position her photos and title, and to soften the focal point image which she then printed out. She added printed and trimmed journaling and monogram textboxes, created with her computer, alongside punched patterned paper circles, stickers and rub-on accents. Christine trimmed the entire layout to a size slightly smaller than 8½" x 11" (22cm x 28cm), and then adhered it to a sheet of patterned paper for a hint of border and emphasis.

Supplies: Patterned paper (7 Gypsies, Scenic Route Paper Co.); rub-ons (Scenic Route Paper Co.); stickers (Provo Craft, Scenic Route Paper Co.); punches (Family Treasures); image editing software (Adobe); photo paper; cardstock

FABULOUS FIRST GRADE GROWTH

HEATHER PRECKEL
SWANNANOA, NORTH CAROLINA

With Hello Kitty backpack and lunchbox in tow, Heather's daughter set off for her first day of first grade, celebrated on this festive creation incorporating many memories. Heather used her computer to gather and print out the highlights of the day in 2½" x 2½" (6cm x 6cm) format, which she then placed as a photo border around her layout. She used a corner rounder on her photo border, and handwrote her journaling around the entire layout in the open border. Rub-on letters and colorful buttons establish the title embellished with an assortment of ribbons on a cardstock block, which Heather raised on foam adhesives for dynamic dimension.

Supplies: Cardstock; ribbons (May Arts, Michaels, Offray); buttons (Junkitz); rub-ons (Creative Imaginations); pen; foam spacer

BIG day

holly

age: just turned 5 a week ago
starting: "TK" (Transitional Kindergarten)
teacher: Mrs. Branderhorst
hours: 8:30am – 11:30am

drew

age: will turn 7 in two weeks
starting: First Grade
teacher: Mrs. Brazil
hours: 8:30am – 3:00pm

The first day of school is always a big deal. But this 'first day' is especially BIG.

Holly, you are moving from the preschool to the elementary school. This means a more structured and education-focused day, and you change buildings to where all the big kids go to school! Drew, you are starting first grade, which means you will be going to school all day for the first time. Instead of getting out at 11:30am, you will be in school until 3:00pm!

This year is also the first year of the new dress code policy. The parents voted and an overwhelming majority said "yes" to school uniforms. I have to say, as a mommy, I love the idea and think you both look adorable in your crisp white shirts and blue uniform attire.

I will miss you both as you go off to your first day of school today. Looks like even Phileaux the cat will too!

September 7, 2004

BIG DAY

KATHLEEN SUMMERS
ROSEVILLE, CALIFORNIA

Holly and big brother Drew's Big Day marks the first of many big changes this dynamic duo will embrace together this year. Kathleen kept the look of her layout as crisp and clean as her children's school uniforms, utilizing very little embellishment. Kathleen stamped her title letters using a combination of glimmer chalk and chalk enhancer rather than stamping ink. She mixed the two together and then applied to the stamp right before pressing. The mix was also used in stamping lowercase names onto her children's personal info blocks, as well as the alphabet she created on patterned paper at the right.

Supplies: Patterned paper (My Mind's Eye); stamps (Sugarloaf Products); glimmer chalk, chalk enhancer (Craf-T); photo corners (Heidi Swapp); pen; cardstock

THE WALK IN

ANGIE HEAD
FRIENDSWOOD, TEXAS

What could be more comforting on a walk into kindergarten than the hand of a close friend? Angie designed this layout around the fun and growth her daughter will gain throughout the school year, using a large, realistic sticker at the top to focus on the joy of learning. She cut large, coordinating, cardstock circles for her background, and overlaid letter stickers for her title. A decorative rub-on was placed along her focal-point image for an elegant edge, while rounded corners on all photos give a warm and friendly softness to the page. Ribbons and flowers add further feminine frill, alongside hand-cut file folders for the perfect thematic journaling blocks.

Supplies: Border sticker, letter stickers (Bo-Bunny Press); ribbon (Doodlebug Design, Making Memories, May Arts); flowers (Michaels, Prima); rub-ons (Creative Imaginations); brads; circle cutter; corner rounder; solvent ink; pen; cardstock

1ST DAY ANTICIPATION

CAROLINE HUOT
LAVAL, QUEBEC, CANADA

Even though Caroline's son talked with anticipation for months on end about his first full day of kindergarten, this tell-tale image of her son's nervous hands reveals a hint of apprehension. Caroline enlarged the photo of the bus to 5¾" x 12" (15cm x 30cm) with photo-editing software, which she also used to create a gentle haze around its edges for greater focus on the bus. She journaled directly onto the bottom of the photo with pen. On the photo of her son, Caroline punched tiny holes around her son's hands for greater emphasis relative to the journaling. Caroline chose patterned papers that complement her photos, and drew out the yellows by adding actual pencils as embellishments, sanded in half for less bulk.

Supplies: Patterned paper (BasicGrey); letter stickers (Paper Loft); hole punch (Making Memories); pencils; black pen; cardstock

FLASH CARD SET

BRENDA MCANDREWS
VILLA HILLS, KENTUCKY

A colorful set of flashcards serves double duty as a fun learning tool and a memory keepsake. Brenda trimmed various colored cardstocks into circles, inked the edges for definition and added a medley of square-punched patterned papers to bring out the harmonious hues in her photos. She added small handmade labels constructed of white cardstock and mini brads to identify each color. A large jump ring fastens the cards together and is accented with a pretty rainbow of ribbons.

Supplies: Patterned paper (American Crafts, Autumn Leaves, BasicGrey, Bazzill, Creative Imaginations, KI Memories, Paper Patch, Paper Pizazz, Rusty Pickle); bookring; ribbons (source unknown); brads (Creative Impressions, Doodlebug Designs); square punch; cardstock; Jill font (Font Garden)

1ST DAY OF PRESCHOOL JITTERS

KIM MORENO
TUCSON, ARIZONA

Kim created this layout to capture the nervousness of her son balanced out by the confidence of his sister. Kim double-matted the focal-point photo for greater impact, and single-matted the accent images. She cut the number strip from patterned paper and attached with paper clips to the page, which are balanced by paper clip accents in the upper right. She printed her journaling onto a transparency, using a letter sticker to begin, and then added coordinating letter stickers in her multi-media title, which also includes chipboard letters, and stamps.

Supplies: Patterned paper (KI Memories, Three Bugs in a Rug); letter stickers (Scenic Route Paper Co.); chipboard letters, leather corner accent (Making Memories); chipboard shapes (Heidi Swapp); letter stamps (EK Success, PSX Design); paperclips; pigment ink; cardstock

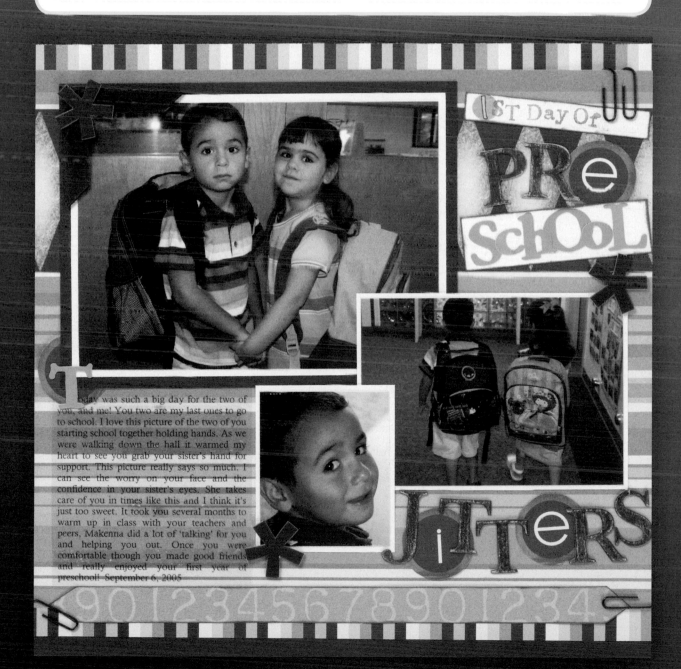

STOP, DROP & READ

BARB PFEFFER
OMAHA, NEBRASKA

One of Alexandra's favorite events of first grade was the Stop, Drop and Read days, where students were required to carry a book at all times and read at unexpected times. Barb created this calm and reflective page of her daughter's love for literature by layering blocks of patterned paper on her background, rounding several of the corners. She added chipboard letters in her title for depth, and gave texture to the page by tying a ribbon through a bookmark tag, set behind the focal-point photo.

Supplies: Patterned paper (Creative Imaginations); chipboard letters, tag (K & Company); letter stickers (BasicGrey); ribbon (May Arts); corner rounder; cardstock

PHOTO CHECKLIST

* ★ First teacher
* ★ First day of school emotions
* ★ First backpack/lunchbox and contents
* ★ Favorite school subjects
* ★ A day in the life
* ★ First friendships
* ★ Traveling to and from school
* ★ Holidays and special events at school
* ★ Blossoming talents
* ★ Life skills learned: tying shoes, zipping zippers, buttoning buttons, etc.
* ★ School bus adventures
* ★ Keepsake artwork and first attempts at writing letters, names, numbers, etc.
* ★ Afterschool activities

One of your favorite events at school this year was the Stop, Drop & Read days. On these days, students are required to carry a book with them at all times. When the announcement comes, you must stop what you are doing, get your book, sit down and read. What a great method to promote reading in a fun way!

LEARNING TO READ

ANGIE HEAD
FRIENDSWOOD, TEXAS

The milestone moment of learning to read is captured in these heart-warming images of Angie passing on the literary torch to her daughter. Angie cut patterned papers in country-charm prints for a layered nostalgic look, inking the edges for aged effect. She created her title circle with letter stickers, and embellished it with ribbons flowing across and onto a wooden frame accent offset by a silk flower. Angie furthered the theme by adding tags for her journaling and decorative rub-ons, which she connected with rivets and ribbons for a hinged, open-book effect.

Supplies: Patterned paper (My Mind's Eye); rub-ons (BasicGrey, Creative Imaginations); chalk ink (Clearsnap); letter stickers (Creative Imaginations, My Mind's Eye); ribbon (Making Memories); rivets, wooden frame (Chatterbox); brad; silk flower (source unknown); pen; cardstock

First Grade · he has such a good time doing it! · Painting, · cutting, gluing, coloring, drawing, glitter, Play doh, etc. · Jonathan loves art class. It doesn't matter what the project is... · His motto ... · "the messier it is, the better!" · Art Class

ART

SHARON LAAKKONEN
SUPERIOR, WISCONSIN

No matter the project or the medium, Jonathan loves art class, with his motto being, "the messier it is, the better!" Shannon created this page to showcase Jonathan's passion, with images of him hard at play, and actual artwork he created incorporated into the design. Shannon used vibrant, playful colors and patterns found in swatches of paper, and set the paper strips around the border of her photos to journal around them. Acrylic flowers form colorful opposing angles in the center of the design, while acrylic translucent letters convey the theme and title.

Supplies: Patterned paper (American Crafts, Prima, Provo Craft); acrylic flowers (Queen & Co.); acrylic letters (KI Memories); file tabs (Imagination Project); notebook paper; thread; pen; dye ink; corner rounder; cardstock

SUPERSTAR

KATHLEEN SUMMERS
ROSEVILLE, CALIFORNIA

A proud day for Kathleen's daughter, Holly, shines from this star-studded layout, celebrating the honor of receiving a highly sought after award at her school. Playing up the celestial theme, Kathleen added dimension to the page by creating wax star embellishments. Ribbons lend the look of shooting stars while creating textural fun.

Supplies: Patterned paper (Die Cuts With A View); chipboard label, chipboard stars, rhinestones (Heidi Swapp); star stamps (Sugarloaf Products); acrylic paint; glitter glue; distress ink; beeswax (Yaley); ribbon (American Crafts); clear embossing enamel; pen; cardstock; Just Plain Little font (Two Peas in a Bucket)

CREATE EMBELLISHMENTS USING WAX AND STAMPS

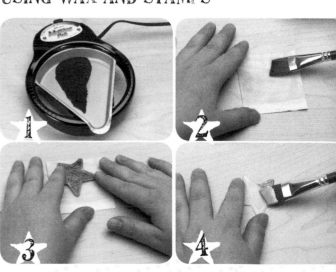

[1] MELT NATURAL BEESWAX IN A MELTING POT AT 180° F (82° C).
[2] USING AN OLD PAINTBRUSH, APPLY COATS OF BEESWAX TO LIGHT-COLORED CARDSTOCK. [3] HEAT BEESWAX WITH A HEAT GUN TO SOFTEN, AND PRESS STAMP INTO WAX. [4] WHEN WAX IS COOL, PULL STAMP FROM WAX. TRIM AROUND EDGE OF DESIGN, AND PAINT AS DESIRED.

Sophie had cousin Emily decorate her hair for crazy hair day at preschool. Once she got to school, she was completely humiliated and hid in the corner. Soon Ms. Fran came to the rescue by taking most of it out and Sophie was happy and ran off with her friends.

April 1, 2005

CRAZY HAIR DAY HUMILIATION

SUZY PLANTAMURA
LAGUNA NIGUEL, CALIFORNIA

Sophie's crazy hairstyle for her preschool's Crazy Hair Day turned out to be a little too crazy for her own pride and fashion sense. Suzy's touching layout uses a vertical grid of 2" x 2" (5cm x 5cm) photos showcasing the festive hairdo at varying angles, and capturing the humiliated expressions of the model. The image of the compassionate teacher was changed to black and white to stand apart from the other photos and to coordinate with the color palette. Playing up the "crazy" theme, Suzy cut a curvy edge along a wild pink paisley print background paper. Her title is a mix of rub-ons and handwritten letters that she enhanced with colored pencils.

Supplies: Patterned paper (Mara Mi); rub-on letters, metal accent (KI Memories); buttons (Autumn Leaves); embroidery floss, ribbon (source unknown); staples; solvent ink; pen; image editing software (Adobe); cardstock

AMAZING DAYS

CHRISTINE TRAVERSA
JOLIET, ILLINOIS

Hard work and dedication are concepts 5-year-old Rylie embraces when it comes to her passion for gymnastics! Christine created this special page using a combination of computer programs and traditional paper methods to encourage her daughter's dreams of someday becoming an Olympic gymnast. Using image-editing software, Christine positioned her photos and added pinstriping and title elements. She then printed out this portion of the design and added stickers, patterned paper strips and diecuts. After trimming to a size just shy of 8½" x 11" (22cm x 28cm), she mounted the entire page to cardstock.

Supplies: Patterned paper, die-cuts (Scenic Route Paper Co.); stickers (EK Success); image editing software (Adobe); photo paper

Rylie, for a 5 year old, your life is pretty exciting! You do gymnastics almost every day of the week! And, it shows! Your dedication to the sport is outstanding! You tell me you want to be an Olympic gymnast when you grow up, and I believe you! Keep it up, Ry, and you will go far!

OUR MORNING ROUTINE

HEATHER PRECKEL
SWANNANOA, NORTH CAROLINA

While her mornings may seem like a groggy blur of waking up one moment and then finding herself at school the next, Kiersten's mommy created this clever collage layout to fill in the blanks of the morning routine. Heather took numerous photos throughout a typical morning, and then printed them into a collage format and mounted it onto an inked cardstock mat. She cut a large, playfully-patterned circle to set behind the collage, giving the illusion of a clock to add to the theme. Patterned cotton art tape strips lend festive flair to the borders, and repeat the look of the printed journaling strips.

Supplies: Patterned paper, chipboard letters, cotton art tape (Imagination Project); brads (Junkitz); dye ink; pen; cardstock; Flea Market font (Two Peas in a Bucket)

LOVE NOTES

JESSIE BALDWIN
LAS VEGAS, NEVADA

What could be more precious to a mother's heart than handwritten love notes from her child? Spraying actual notes from her daughter, Violet, with both a preserving spray to keep them intact and an acid free spray to protect the page, Jessie set them over the edge of her focal-point photo. Jessie used cool, coordinating colors throughout the layout, allowing the stark white paper from the notes to stand at attention, while balancing the overall composition with perfectly positioned white acrylic flowers. A photo border creates a dynamic linear impact along the bottom of the page, which is repeated throughout in the look of running ribbons.

Supplies: Cardstock; plastic letters (KI Memories); opaque flowers, brads (Queen & Co.); clear flowers (Heidi Swapp); ribbons (May Arts, Maya Road, Offray); notebook paper; pen; acid-free spray, page protector spray (Krylon)

KID CITY

KATHY FESMIRE
ATHENS, TENNESSEE

As Isaac entered Mrs. Carol's kindergarten class, as the third of Kathy's children to have this special teacher, Kathy designed this special tribute page to commemorate the occasion and this beloved family friend. By converting the photo to black and white, she gained the freedom to choose the bright and lively green color scheme for a lighthearted feel, which she enhanced through dancing patterns and whimsical accents. Using a kid-inspired font, the journaling was uniquely written as a letter from Isaac to his teacher. Large wooden letters set over the textural mesh background add a dramatic strength to the title, while also lending dimension.

Supplies: Patterned paper (My Mind's Eye); chipboard letters (Heidi Swapp); wooden letters, buttons (source unknown); leather flowers, photo corners (Making Memories); letter stickers (EK Success); decorative mesh (Magic Mesh); distress ink; acrylic paint; ribbons (Offray); cardstock

HAVE FUN WITH WORDS

Make your scrapbook journaling spifferific by adding playful nonsense words or by using rhyme. Do you know the meaning of words such as balderdash, flapdoodle, flobbergobber, ketchallicious and yurp? Say them out loud and your child is sure to have a case of the simples (uncontrollable giggles). Look to these sources for inspiration:

★ Song lyrics
★ Nursery rhymes
★ Children's literature
★ Writings of well-loved authors such as Lewis Carroll and Theodor Seuss Geisel (Dr. Seuss)
★ Online dictionaries or word-related resources

MRS. CAROL,

i can't believe i get to be in your room this year! morgan, hayden and mommy have all told me how great you are. i feel so lucky to be the third person in our family to have you as a kindergarten teacher. kid city, here i come!!!

Love,
Isaac

WICKEDLY CUTE

BARBARA PFEFFER
OMAHA, NEBRASKA

All dressed up with somewhere to go, Barbara's daughter and her friend pose as they prepare to go onstage as the most glamorous wicked stepsisters Cinderella has ever encountered! In her journaling block, Barbara shares the humorous account of finding the perfect dresses for their parts. Hand-cut swirls of patterned paper enhance the design as they waltz among the page elements. Her title was created using a combination of rub-on and sticker letters, set along the upper dancing swirl, while chipboard hearts add simplistic charm. Rhinestones give the final finesse to the layout, embellishing the title and crown details.

Supplies: Patterned paper, chipboard hearts (Fiskars); rub-ons, photo corner punch (EK Success); letter stickers (American Crafts); rhinestones (K & Company); cardstock; Peachy Keen font (Two Peas in a Bucket)

For the first grade school plays, Lexi was given the part of Stepsister #2 in Cinderella, while her friend Morgan was Stepsister #1. Morgan's mom and I had to laugh at how they both focused on their costumes. They wanted the prettiest, fanciest gowns possible. Lexi's had to be pink because of her line "Cinderella, my pink dress must be hemmed. Go get it at once!" Morgan's had to be blue because of a similar line.

We had some trouble finding a suitable pink gown, until at last Lexi spotted one at Dillard's. I gulped at the $52 price tag, but she was head over heels in love, and I just couldn't deny her. Morgan on the other hand had a blue flower girl dress to use, but she insisted it needed fancying up with as much tulle as possible. Neither Tanya nor I thought the stepsisters should overshadow the star of the show, but what can we say? With two such wickedly cute girls playing the parts, the stepsisters had to step out in their finest!

May 11, 2006

FACTS MASTER

KIM MORENO
TUCSON, ARIZONA

A geometric playground is the only way to describe a layout fit for a Math Facts Master! Kim had fun with the page design, incorporating large circles formed with a circle cutter, punched stars from patterned paper (matted for emphasis), and a large, rectangular photo of her beaming Facts Master, which she double matted to stand out. Using a masculine color scheme throughout the layout, Kim painted her title chipboard letters to coordinate, finishing with a glossy coat for shimmer and shine to match the pride in her son's eyes.

Supplies: Patterned paper (Three Bugs in a Rug); chipboard letters (Heidi Swapp); star punch (Marvy); circle cutter; stamps (Ma Vinci Reliquary); acrylic paint; brads; hole punch; 3-D gloss medium (Ranger); pen; cardstock

THE KINDERGARTEN PICNIC AND BASIC MATH

KITTY FOSTER
SNELLVILLE, GEORGIA

Close-up images and action shots plus alphabet, tablet and apple-themed papers equal the perfect balance of high-energy fun and festivity in Kitty's layout about her son's kindergarten picnic. She used the alphabet paper to cut out the letters for her title and subtitle, and printed descriptive words from the photos onto cut-out patterned paper apples for a playful addition to the page.

Supplies: Patterned paper (Bo-Bunny Press); rub-ons (BasicGrey); chalk ink; cardstock

treasure hunt

Turkey feathers! What? Who let a turkey roam around the park grounds? Well, it seems Sahuaro Ranch park has quite a collection of turkeys so there were plenty of feathers lying around waiting to be discovered.

The Preschool Treasure Hunt was a huge success from the minute the children entered the park. Harry and Ethan had the best time gathering treasures and tucking them in their little white lunch bags. Lift the flaps to see what they found!

CREATE CIRCULAR FOLDER TABS

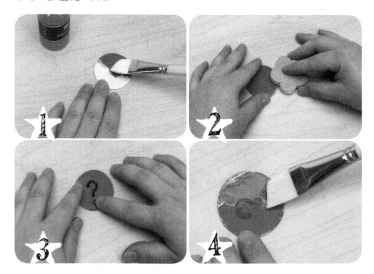

[1] USING A PAINTBRUSH, APPLY ACRYLIC PAINT ONTO COASTER OR CHIPBOARD CIRCLE. ALLOW TO DRY. [2] DISTRESS CHIPBOARD WITH SANDPAPER. [3] ADHERE LETTER STICKER. [4] APPLY ONE COAT OF DIMENSIONAL GLAZE TO ADD SHINE.

TREASURE HUNT

KIM KESTI
PHOENIX, ARIZONA

Pinecones, sticks and turkey feathers were just a few of the favorite treasures hunted down by the students in her sons' preschool during this discovery-centered event. Playing up the theme of hidden treasure in her layout, Kim attached several of her photos from the day on file folders, which open up to reveal journaling buried inside.

Supplies: Patterned paper, coasters, cotton art tape, fabric strips (Imagination Project); letter stickers (Doodlebug Designs); rub-on (Autumn Leaves); diamond glaze (Judikins); acrylic paint (Making Memories); cardstock; Arial font (Microsoft)

GINGERBREAD HOUSE

KATHY FESMIRE
ATHENS, TENNESSEE

Christmastime in Isaac's classroom means it's time for the exciting tradition of decorating gingerbread houses. Kathy kept her page design simple, allowing the focus to be kept on the photos of her son's pride at his creation, yet she did maintain a vibrant energy by employing bright colors and quick snippets of bold, thematic patterns. A small, holiday-themed license plate attached to the page with ribbons adds boyish charm with simplicity. Rub-ons, candy themed stickers, wire, ribbon and foam dots form a fun and colorful title.

Supplies: Patterned paper (EK Success, Provo Craft); rub-ons (Karen Foster Design, Making Memories); title tag (Westrim); ribbon (Offray); stickers, 3-D dots (EK Success); paint (Plaid); cardstock

LIFE'S
CHRISTMAS
MOMENTS

Making Gingerbread houses is a classroom tradition in Kid City. Isaac couldn't wait to get his hands on the candy and decorate his house. His little Teddy Graham friend came knocking on the door, and one even made it on top of the house. When I asked him what the bear was doing up there he said "He is a roofer". How on earth does he come up with these things??

gingerbread house

december

SPOTLIGHT

CAROLINE HUOT
LAVAL, QUEBEC, CANADA

What an honor for Caroline to be brought in by her son for his special Show-n-Tell Week, being "in the spotlight" at school! Designing her layout around the week's theme, Caroline arranged her cropped circle photos to increase in size, creating the illusion of a spotlight. The matted, cropped photos also allowed Caroline to keep the focus of each image on the subjects, without all the busy background distractions. Strips of patterned number and letter papers help convey the classroom setting, while punched stars arranged around the images emphasize her "star" son featured in the spotlight.

Supplies: Patterned paper (Three Bugs in a Rug, KI Memories); letter stickers (Chatterbox); star punch (source unknown); circle cutter; cardstock

Each week in your class, a child is in the spotlight. When it was your turn, you brought your favourite books, toys, medals and pictures. You also brought ME. You wanted me to show and talk about scrapbooking. Your classmates were captivated and by the looks of it, you were proud to have me there. You were happy to show the page you did, also. It certainly was the highlight of your spotlight week! Week of November 21ˢᵗ 2005

For Violet's 100th day of school she had to bring in one hundred things to share with the class. She chose her favorite cereal— Cheerios— and counted them out herself.

What a big girl!

100TH DAY

JESSIE BALDWIN
LAS VEGAS, NEVADA

For Violet's 100th day of school, she had to bring in one hundred items to share with her class. Jessie celebrated the event with this cheerful page, showcasing photos of Violet with one hundred pieces of her favorite cereal. Jessie began by adding warmth to the page, arranging 3" (8cm) squares of coordinating patterned papers into a quilt-style grid. She mounted her images onto cardstock, adhered it to the page, and then journaled on coordinating paper, which she cut into strips. Her bold title was created by combining stamped numbers with sanded chipboard letters.

Supplies: Patterned paper (Scrapworks); chipboard letters (Pressed Petals); dye ink; stamps (Technique Tuesday); gel pen; cardstock

TEACHER THANK YOU

LISA DIXON
EAST BRUNSWICK, NEW JERSEY

Lisa wanted to express her gratitude to her young children's kindergarten and first grade teachers, but wanted to do so in a truly unique and original way. Using an online tutorial, Lisa went *back to school* to learn an origami paper folding technique to fashion custom paper flowers out of patterned paper and floral wire. She embellished a small glass vase accented with ribbon and a gift tag and included a packet of Zinnia Thumbelina seeds tucked into a vellum envelope along with the popular children's book *Planting a Rainbow* by Lois Ehlert (Harcourt, Inc.).

Supplies: Patterned paper, tag (Chatterbox); ribbon (Beaux Regards, Chatterbox); acrylic paint; dye ink; distress ink; shapable thread (Scrapworks); blank card (The Paper Cut); origami folding directions (Expert Village); seed packet; glass bottle; floral wire; floral tape; glassine envelope; children's book

This was a difficult goodbye for us. Mrs. Wilson had not only been your kindergarten teacher but also Morgan and Madison's. Mrs. Wilson has become a close family friend and has done so much for us throughout the years we were in Germany. Mrs. Wilson has especially done a lot for you Mitchell. In the beginning of the year I remember telling her that you are different from the other two in a jokingly manner. Well several months into the school year she started noticing differences too. We decided to have you tested. Well they ran you through the whole gamut of tests and concluded that you had mild Aspergers and were a very gifted little boy. We always knew you were a smart kid and a little quirky, that was just the Mitchell we loved. I thank Mrs. Wilson for seeing this in you. As a family we miss Mrs. Wilson everyday. I love this picture of the two of you, I was able to capture her love for you and yours for her. June 16, 2005

special **memories**

Saying **GOODBYE**

SAYING GOODBYE

KIM MORENO
TUCSON, ARIZONA

Kim used a single large, double-matted photo to focus on the special bond her son, Mitchell, shared with his kindergarten teacher. Beneath the image and journaling block, she layered patterned papers, which coordinated with the shirts in the photograph. Kim then attached a market tag directly to the photo with an oversized brad embellished with a rub-on heart. Chipboard letters at the bottom overlaid with a printed transparency create a dramatic title block.

Supplies: Patterned paper (Paper Salon); chipboard letters (Pressed Petals); chipboard bookplate (Everlasting Keepsakes); metal accent (Making Memories); brads (Bazzill, Making Memories); heart charms (Doodlebug Design); embroidery floss; market tag (Pebbles); rub-ons (Autumn Leaves); cardstock

MY RISING STAR

HEATHER PRECKEL
SWANNANOA,
NORTH CAROLINA

Heather created this stellar design to celebrate a unique "graduation" ceremony at her daughter's school. Heather incorporated the star theme from the ceremony into her layout by using double-sided tape to create the star shape overtop her photos, to which she then adhered neutral-colored buttons. Her title was set directly onto the focal photo as well, using a white pen and rub-on letters. A report card element and star-themed sticker continue the theme, along with stars drawn by hand around the inked computer journaling strips.

Supplies: Patterned paper, report card (7 Gypsies); buttons, brads (Junkitz); sticker (Autumn Leaves); rub-ons (Making Memories); pen; dye ink; cardstock; font (Two Peas in a Bucket)

SERIOUSLY?

KATHLEEN SUMMERS
ROSEVILLE, CALIFORNIA

Here on Kathleen's all-too-familiar page of parental dilemma, a mother's utter disbelief at the pomp and circumstance surrounding her four-year-old's Preschool Graduation turns to sheer adoration in a heartbeat when she sees how cute her daughter looks in her cap and gown. Allowing the single commemorative photo to keep the spotlight, she balances the formal look with lighthearted, handwritten journaling on textured cardstock. Kathleen used metallic rub-ons to shade the highlighted word boxes in her journaling, while pink acrylic flowers and floral corner rub-ons add pretty pizzazz.

Supplies: Cardstock; sticker letters (K & Company); patterned tape, ghost flowers (Heidi Swapp); corner rub-ons (BasicGrey); metallic rub-ons (Craft-T); mini brads (source unknown); photo corners; pen

LEAPIN' LEPRECHAUNS!

KITTY FOSTER
SNELLVILLE, GEORGIA

Forget March coming in like a lion. It's the leprechauns you need to worry about, as Kitty's son learned from his kindergarten St. Patrick's Day celebration! To create this lucky layout, Kitty printed her journaling at the bottom of orange paper, which she cut into a wave for playfulness at the top. She mounted her photos onto patterned green paper which she then set overtop the orange, embellished with the necklace from the photos. Rub-on letters form a flowing title along the curve of her paper, and shamrocks cut from the March-themed background paper provide simplistic flair and additional journaling details.

Supplies: Patterned paper (Karen Foster Design); rub-ons (Junkitz); chalk ink; hand-cut shamrocks; necklace accent (source unknown)

TWO WHEELER

JESSIE BALDWIN
LAS VEGAS, NEVADA

The milestone moment of every childhood is celebrated here on Jessie's free-wheeling design, which cherishes her daughter's transition to riding a bike minus training wheels. Jessie took her inspiration from a magazine ad, layering loads of images onto the page, surrounded by whimsical, carefree doodles created with white and pink pens. Fabric flowers scattered about the page lend texture and feminine festivity, while a decorative, painted metal strip gives an industrial edge to play up the theme.

Supplies: Patterned paper (Prism); letter stickers (Mrs. Grossman's); fabric flowers (Michael Miller); rub-on letters, metal accent strip (Making Memories); acrylic paint; pigment ink; gel pen; page protector spray (Krylon)

CHAPTER 2

THE WHEELS ON THE BUS

[Grades 2 – 5]

Second through fifth grade is the time when life simply doesn't get much better. Your child is discovering who he or she is in all authenticity, no holds barred. Childhood is at its finest these school years: school is still someplace to look forward to going each day; a red striped shirt and purple polka-dot pants make a fine outfit; baths are for wimps; and cootie infestations are in epidemic proportion. Parents may feel a little more settled with the back-to-school routine, yet still stand in awe at the many ways your not-so-little child is growing in stature, knowledge and wisdom. Cling to these moments of Little League, gymnastics, first book reports and best friends. For this is the calm before the storm! Cherish these elementary school days in pages filled with sugar and spice and everything nice, snips and snails and puppy dog tails—for that is what childhood memories should be made of.

ON MY WAY

CHRISTINE TRAVERSA
JOLIET, ILLINOIS

While many students dread the end of summer vacation, Christine's daughter, Karlie, was filled with overwhelming excitement about getting back to buddies, books and the basics. Christine positioned her photos and added cheerful pinstripe elements to the page design using computer software. She printed out the basic layout, mounted it on 8½" x 11" (22cm x 28cm) cardstock, and then added decorative, thematic, photo-real stickers for color and fun. She printed out a colored journaling box created on her computer, and adhered it to her layout.

Supplies: Photo paper; stickers (Cloud 9 Design); brads; image editing software (Adobe); Century Gothic, Times New Roman fonts (Microsoft)

SCRAPBOOKING WITH KIDS

Next time you're at the craft table, invite your little artist to join in the fun. You may be surprised at how much you can inspire a young mind. And chances are you have a surplus of patterned papers, stickers and die cuts just begging to be used. Whether he or she is crafty with crayons or playful with paste, your child will marvel at the creative possibilities. Here are some creations he or she may want to try:

* ★ A traditional scrapbook page
* ★ Birthday party invitations or Valentine's Day cards
* ★ Artist or classmate trading cards
* ★ Baseball or other sports-related cards featuring teammates from school
* ★ Artwork to be framed or included in mini album

HEADING OFF TO 5TH GRADE

CAROLINE HUOT
LAVAL, QUEBEC, CANADA

You can almost hear the squeaking bus doors open here on Caroline's back-to-school design, which laments her son heading into fifth grade and the wings of independence that come with it. She arranged the page to take on the shape of the school bus, rounding her yellow-orange paper into the form and then detailing it with a black cardstock arrow, which pulls the eye toward the second part of her title. Black and orange brads give the page pizzazz and augment the bus-effect with the look of lights. Orange photo anchors balance the look by establishing a visual triangle with the groupings of brads.

Supplies: Patterned paper (KI Memories); number sticker (American Crafts); letter stickers (EK Success); rub-ons (Bobarbo, Imagination Project); photo anchors (Making Memories); brads; corner rounder; pigment ink; cardstock; Garamouche font (Internet download)

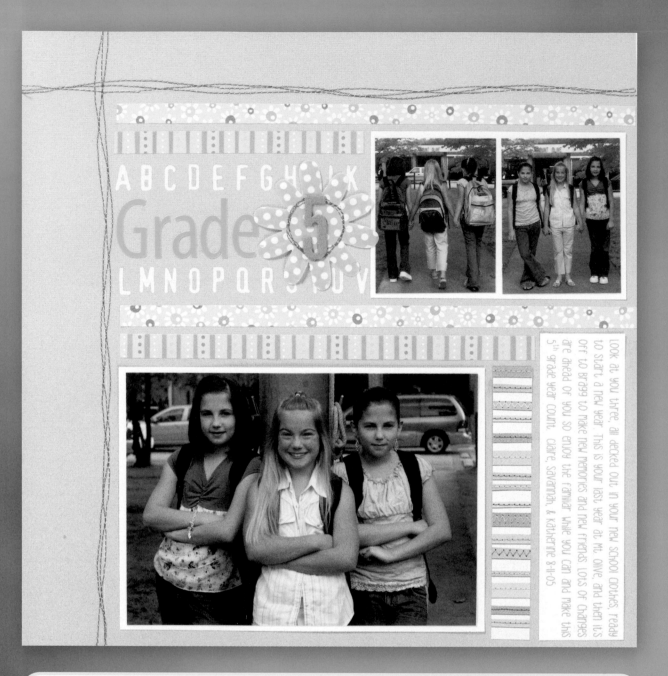

GRADE 5

VANESSA HUDSON
MT. OLIVE, ALABAMA

Girly and glamorous patterned-paper strips meet up with the style and sophistication this fifth grade trio brings to Vanessa's layout, commemorating the girls' last year at their elementary school. Vanessa created a color-blocked style by piecing together the festive paper strips along with her photos, journaling and title block. Her title stands alone as a dynamic element, created with rub-on alphabet letters and letter stickers combined with a chipboard number set overtop a patterned paper flower. Swirling machine stitches around the edges give an energetic border to the page, which adds to the celebratory feel.

Supplies: Patterned paper, flower, letter stickers (Doodlebug Design); chipboard number (Heidi Swapp); rub-ons (KI Memories); thread; cardstock

BACK TO SCHOOL SHOPPING

BARB PFEFFER
OMAHA, NEBRASKA

The smile lighting up this page, due to bags of brand name attire, means back-to-school shopping has arrived for Barb's little fashionista. This tradition-inspired layout employs bright and bold colors for a lively, fun look, while patterned paper circles and a cardstock arc capture the happy, effervescent personality of the page. Barbara punched holes into the title arc and backed the curve with contrasting cardstock. She pulled the title together with a combination of rub-on, sticker and chipboard letters accentuated with ribbon. The layout is completed by a ribbon accessory belting off the bottom border, tying in with the top.

Supplies: Patterned paper, letter stickers, ribbon (Arctic Frog); rub-on letters (Scrapworks); chipboard letters (Pressed Petals); chipboard shapes (Bazzill, Maya Road); acrylic paint; hole punch; circle cutter; cardstock; Delightful font (Lettering Delights)

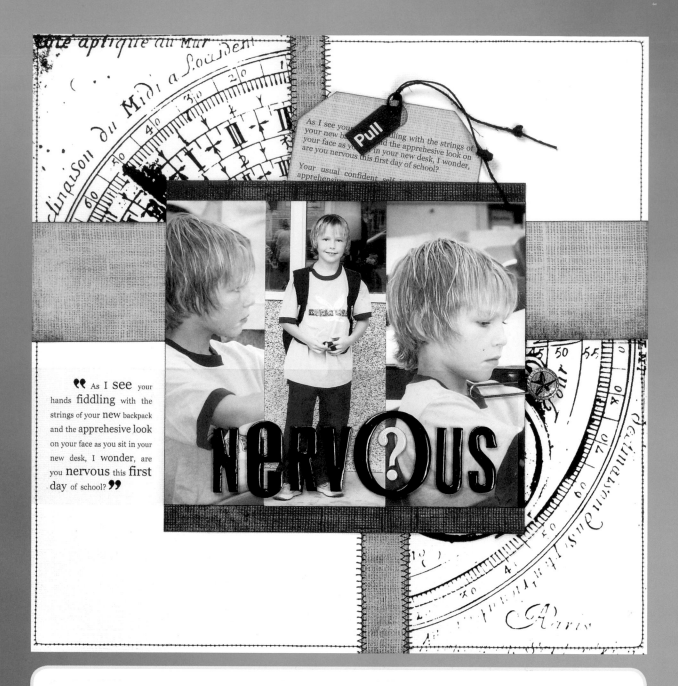

As I see your hands fiddling with the strings of your new backpack and the apprehesive look on your face as you sit in your new desk, I wonder, are you nervous this first day of school?

NERVOUS

AMBER BALEY
WAUPUN, WISCONSIN

By capturing the wringing hands and apprehensive expression on her normally self-assured son, Amber's layout reveals an anxious moment anyone can relate to. Wanting to play up the theme while intriguing the reader further, she selected an excerpt from her pull-out journaling and incorporated it into the design. She cut patterned transparencies for minimal embellishment on her otherwise graphic layout. She altered the paperclip to coordinate with the transparency, adding cut paper with an adhered rub-on accent, finished with a diamond glaze. Machine stitching and inked black edges lend texture and masculine ruggedness.

Supplies: Patterned paper (BasicGrey); patterned transparency (Creative Imaginations); chipboard letters (Heidi Swapp); paper clip (K & Company); rub-ons (7 Gypsies, BasicGrey); tag (Sizzix); transparency; acrylic paint; solvent ink; cardstock; Georgia font (Dafont)

BACK TO SCHOOL

HEATHER PRECKEL
SWANNANOA, NORTH CAROLINA

Uncomplicated structure is the theme of Heather's layout, focusing on the simplistic sentiments which make the back-to-school event such a milestone moment each year. Heather kept the design crisp and neat, while utilizing fun colors in rub-on title letters and cardstock matting for her journaling strips. The large image of the bus packs a dynamic punch toward the theme, while accent photos of this second-grader heading out highlight the excitement of the day and mesh with the journaling.

Supplies: Patterned paper (Autumn Leaves); brad, twill (Creative Impressions); rub-ons (Me & My Big Ideas); label (Dymo); photo corners; corner rounder; pen; cardstock

THE SCHOOL CHOIR

CHRISTINE TRAVERSA
JOLIET, ILLINOIS

Tradition and technology perform an amazing duet here on Christine's timeless treasure, which showcases her daughter's involvement in her grade school choir. Using her computer, she arranged and edited her photos, and then created her title and journaling. After printing out this foundational piece, Christine added patterned paper to the upper left, and applied rub-on accents for classic beauty. She trimmed the borders slightly and adhered the completed design to black cardstock, creating a border for extra impact.

Supplies: Patterned paper (K & Company); rub-ons (Autumn Leaves, Die Cuts With A View, Fancy Pants Designs); image editing software (Adobe); photo paper; cardstock; Century Gothic font (Microsoft)

the school choir ---- 2006

Karlie, your days are so busy in the school choir. You practice several times a week, and perform in public as well. Recently you gave a solo, singing a song from a Broadway musical. It is so exciting to see you perform! We are so proud of you, and so excited for your future!

UGH...HOMEWORK

KIM MORENO
TUCSON, ARIZONA

For as much as Kim's son despises having homework, his mom loves that he continues to make good grades no matter the subject. Here, Kim emphasizes her son's favorite subject, math, by employing geometric patterns in masculine colors to create a dynamic design. Kim grouped black-matted photos of her son hard at work into a triangular formation, which she then emphasized by weaving patterned paper strips into a large triangle among them. She created her title with black letter stickers, spruced up with a couple of blue letter stickers that she outlined for boldness.

Supplies: Patterned paper (Paper Salon); letter stickers (Chatterbox, Li'l Davis Designs); photo turns (7 Gypsies); brads; metal plaque (Making Memories); dye ink; transparency; pen; cardstock

LOOK WHAT I MADE   VANESSA HUDSON
MT. OLIVE, ALABAMA

Vanessa wanted to showcase her daughter's art in a fun and innovative way. She added jazz and pizzazz to a traditional office clipboard by adhering colorful patterned paper to the front side. Pink and black rickrack, grosgrain ribbon, a mini binder clip and a metal-rimmed tag add a further punch of visual interest, while a quick and easy rub-on title accented with arrow brads balances the lower part of the project. To add the perfect finishing touch, Vanessa placed her little superstar's masterpiece front and center tucked securely under the clip.

Supplies: Patterned paper, rub-ons (Scenic Route Paper Co.); photo turns (7 Gypsies); clipboard, paper clip, metal rimmed tag (office supply store); rickrack (Wrights); ribbon (Textured Trios)

DAILY WRITING

KATHLEEN SUMMERS
ROSEVILLE, CALIFORNIA

The passion for the pen is embraced here on Kathleen's creation, which shares the story of the way her son's second grade teacher helped him find and fuel his gift for writing. She kept the layout simple, including only two patterned papers, allowing the photos and journaling to remain the focus. Kathleen printed her journaling directly onto cardstock that she trimmed to 8½" x 12" (22cm x 30cm). Kathleen played up the writing theme of the layout by adding an index tab containing a portion of the title.

Supplies: Patterned paper (Imagination Project); chipboard letters (Making Memories); letter stamps (Hero Arts); stamping ink; index tab (Heidi Swapp); cardstock

The schedule text on the left layout:

7:15 alarm sounds
7:40 eat Breakfast
7:55 ride to school
8:00 bell rings
8:15 roll call
8:20 daily oral language
9:00 daily oral geography
9:15 bathroom break
10:00 spelling
11:00 reading
11:50 math
12:45 hand sanitizer
12:50 lunch
1:30 bathroom break
1:40 make-up work\read
1:55 Gym
2:40 bell rings
3:00 ride home
Start all over tomorrow and try to make it to Friday. 05\06 School year

at school

AT SCHOOL

VANESSA HUDSON
MT. OLIVE, ALABAMA

The daily grind comes alive on Vanessa's design, dedicated to her daughter's typical school-day schedule. The calm and collected demeanor found in the single black-and-white photo of her daughter at school is carried throughout the page in soothing, cool colors, while the busyness of her jam-packed schedule is reflected in the energetic pattern combinations. After piecing her background together, Vanessa machine-stitched rickrack to several seams for nostalgic charm and playfulness. She further embellished the look and theme by printing out three text circles and stamping in the centers.

Supplies: Patterned paper (BasicGrey); chipboard letters, photo corner (Heidi Swapp); rickrack (Wrights); rubber stamp (Technique Tuesday); thread; dye ink; die-cut circles (source unknown); cardstock.

A TYPICAL DAY IN THIRD GRADE

BARB HOGAN
CINCINNATI, OHIO

Barb's daughter, Shannon, shares the sweet details of the third-grade lifestyle, here on this pretty creation. Barb had Shannon handwrite a typical day's schedule on the attached notepaper, which serves as a treasured memento on the page. She tore the edges around the background alphabet paper to coordinate with the jagged edges of the notebook paper and contrast with the smooth-flowing lines of the floral patterns. Barb cut out flowers from patterned paper and overlapped them around the page on top of other patterns and elements for playful energy.

Supplies: Patterned paper (Chatterbox, Rusty Pickle, Urban Lily); notebook paper; rub-on letters (Imagination Project, Wordsworth); paperclip (Target); pen; cardstock

a TyPicAL day in 3rd grade

notes
6:00 - wake up
8:00 - Catch the Bus
8:30 - school starts
11:30 - Lunch time
2:00 - Recess
3:20 - School ends
4:00 - Snack and Homework
5:00 - TKD class
6:30 - dinner
9:00 - nighty night!

A LESSON IN COMPASSION

KITTY FOSTER
SNELLVILLE, GEORGIA

As Kitty's layout attests, not everything is learned in the classroom. Kitty created her layout to honor and document the growth in character her son gained his fifth grade year, as he stepped up to be a supportive friend to his close buddy diagnosed with cancer. Kitty adhered a ¾" (2cm) L-shaped, striped paper strip onto the black cardstock background, and then added her word border printed onto a ½"(1cm) L-shaped, blue paper strip. She created her title by printing the word *compassion* onto yellow patterned paper and adding rub-on letters to both the paper and her photo. The vibrant colors lend a heroic energy to the page, while creating a contrast with the matted black-and-white photos for impact.

Supplies: Patterned paper (My Mind's Eye); rub-ons (Li'l Davis Designs); stars (source unknown); chalk ink; cardstock

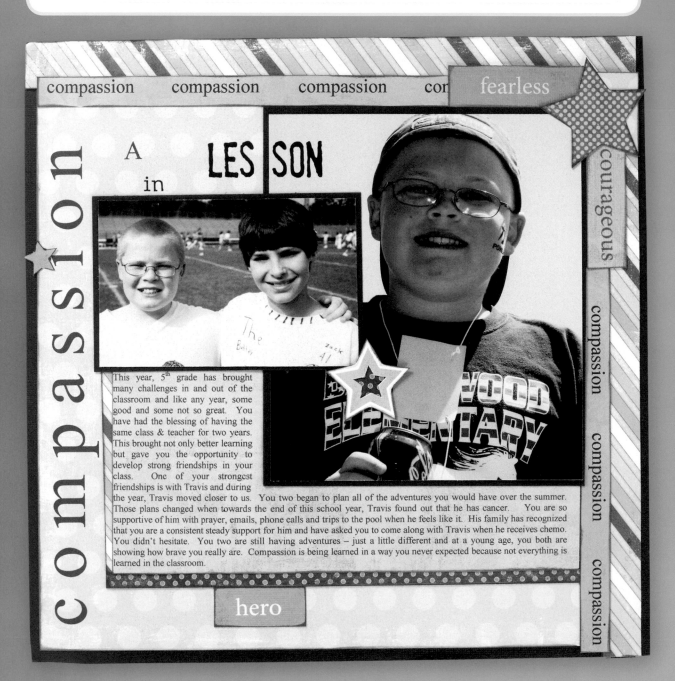

GROWTH CHART

HEATHER PRECKEL
SWANNANOA, NORTH CAROLINA

This decorated tin lunchbox contains a hidden treasure. Heather began by outfitting her tin box in floral patterned paper, checked and polka-dot ribbons and an endearing quote. She then attached white cardstock together to create a five-foot growth chart and folded it accordion-style to fit within the box. Using coordinating patterned paper, she constructed the flower and stem. Circular foot markers, adhered with dimensional adhesive, pop from the flower's stem while stickers, a Dymo label and fanciful ribbons add an additional whimsical touch.

Supplies: Patterned paper (Junkitz); letter stickers (American Crafts); ribbon (May Arts); lunch pail, metal frame (Making Memories); label (Dymo); dye ink; pen; cardstock; Fancy Tree font (Two Peas in a Bucket)

THE ADVENTURES OF FLAT TORIA

BARBARA PFEFFER
OMAHA, NEBRASKA

Barbara's light-hearted layout documents Toria's class project, based on the children's book *Flat Stanley*, and highlights the many adventures had by Toria's 2-D version of herself. After arranging her many photos and two journaling blocks, Barb adhered patterned paper to chipboard circles affixed with die-cut numbers, which she then attached to each accent photo. Corresponding numbers were added to the journaling captions on the right.

Supplies: Patterned paper, chipboard letters, ribbon (We R Memory Keepers); letter stickers (SEI); die-cut numbers (QuicKutz); circle punch; chipboard circles (Imagination Project); brads; chalk ink; cardstock

WEEK AT A GLANCE

JENNIFER GALLACHER
AMERICAN FORK, UTAH

A week in the school life of Jennifer's daughter is documented on this clever calendar page. Jennifer machine-stitched white cardstock and a festive paper strip onto her background, and then added a handmade tab. Punched circles from photos and patterned pages were arranged to lend the look of a weekly calendar page, while yellow acrylic numbers further the effect. Jennifer printed her journaling captions onto white cardstock cut into strips, which she then stitched onto the page as well. Buttons, brads and acrylic letters give this page dimension and charm, while office clips and cardstock checkmarks further the school-time theme.

Supplies: Patterned paper (BasicGrey, Creative Imaginations, Frances Meyer, Karen Foster Design, KI Memories, Making Memories, Provo Craft); letter stickers (Doodlebug Designs); letter stamps (Karen Foster Design) rub-ons (Die Cuts With A View); acrylic letters, numbers and accents (KI Memories); circle punch; pink clip (K & Company); acrylic circle (Heidi Grace Designs); buttons (source unknown); brads; photo corners; pigment ink; thread; cardstock

TY AND ELLIE

DENISE TUCKER
VERSAILLES, INDIANA

Ty has developed a crush on a classmate of his, named Ellie. As soon as Ty gets home from school, the first question out of his mouth is, "Can I call Ellie?" The two of them would talk for hours if we would allow it. They giggle, gab, and laugh, and it's refreshing to see the happiness their friendship brings to Ty

Grade school friendships don't come any sweeter than the one on display here. Denise painted a 12" x 12" (30cm x 30cm) chipboard square with textural paint, which she used a heat gun to speed dry, creating a bubbled appearance. She created the lower border by inking and layering two strips of patterned paper and attaching them to the base. Denise added letter stickers onto diamonds cut from patterned paper and mounted onto chipboard. She then inked and covered them with decoupage. Punched circles attached with foam adhesive spacers give the page a festive feel and allow the images of Ty and Ellie to be the main attraction.

Supplies: Patterned paper, letter stickers (Rusty Pickle); chipboard (Crescent Cardboard Co.); flowers (Making Memories); jumbo brads (Bazzill); buttons (Dress It Up, Making Memories); ribbon (Offray); circle punch; textured paint, photo protector (Krylon), small tag (source unknown), stamp stickers (Wal-Mart); library card (The Designer's Library); decoupage medium; stamping ink; distress ink; staples; pen; cardstock

HOMEWORK TIME
CAROLINE HUOT
LAVAL, QUEBEC, CANADA

There are some things in life you just don't want to do but have to, and for Caroline's fifth grader, that something is homework. Using materials with a school supply theme, Caroline created this quiet and uncluttered page design to capture the atmosphere of her son's homework time. On her cardstock background, she attached ruled paper for her journaling, and then added a 5" x 7" (13cm x 18cm) photo matted onto an opened file folder. Choosing a stamp with a handwriting flair, Caroline created her upper title letters and then used typewriter key stickers for the lower portion.

Supplies: Patterned paper (Scenic Route Paper Co.); notebook paper; file folder (Paper Loft); chipboard bracket (Fancy Pants Designs); brads; labels (Paper Loft, Scrapworks); stamps (FontWerks); letter stickers (EK Success); photo anchors; photo corners; pigment ink; acrylic paint; pen; cardstock

ART EXPO

CAROLINE HUOT
LAVAL, QUEBEC, CANADA

Creativity abounds on Caroline's layout, showcasing her son's teamwork exhibit at his fifth grade Art Expo. Caroline chose a blue, gray and brown color scheme to carry out the look of the castle, and added red accents to emphasize its flag. Inked chipboard letters and fabric tab lend vintage emotion to the layout, while the sanded, inked edges of the photos pull the page together in the same rustic fashion. Wanting to draw more attention to the top right portion of her title, Caroline added the patterned paper arrow, which balances out the bottom border and repeats the tower shape found on the castle itself.

Supplies: Patterned paper (My Mind's Eye); chipboard letters (Pressed Petals); letter stickers (EK Success); fabric tab (7 Gypsies); chipboard circle (Cloud 9 Design); brads; library card (source unknown); dye ink; sandpaper pen; cardstock

ROCKING THE HOUSE

KELLI NOTO
CENTENNIAL, COLORADO

With an arcing title, flying arrows and psychedelic patterns, Kelli's energetic layout revisits her son's first taste of stardom at his elementary school talent show. To arrange her die-cut letters into the title arc, Kelli used a bowl to position the circle shape. She then added die-cut arrows to add to the rock-and-roll excitement of the page, while leading the eye to the accent images. Details of this musical debut were printed onto self-adhesive clear computer paper and simply set in place.

Supplies: Patterned paper (Imagination Project); die-cut letters and shapes (QuicKutz); self-adhesive clear computer paper (ChartPak); cardstock

SOCCER SEASON

KIM MORENO
TUCSON, ARIZONA

A year in pictures testifies to the explosive talent in Kim's son, and serves as a milestone by which to gauge his progress on the soccer field. The soccer theme is magnified on Kim's design by coordinating a collection of circles, from patterned papers, cut-out prints and chipboard borders, that repeat the shape of the ball and convey a kinesthetic flow. The variation in her title, between upper and lowercase painted chipboard letters, scores a dynamic play on the page, as does the bold journaling circle enhanced by inked, printed journaling strips.

Supplies: Patterned paper, photo turns (Junkitz); chipboard letters (Magistical Memories, Scenic Route Paper Co.); chipboard accents (Magistical Memories) stamps (FontWerks); number brads (Queen & Co.); brads; cardstock

only one kid could be WACKY, WILD, and WEIRD enough to be WILLY WONKA in the school play—and that was Kyle Novak!!

May 2006

PLAY
BILBRAY ELEMENT

STAMPED RESIST TECHNIQUE

[1] STAMP CIRCLES ONTO RED CARDSTOCK STRIP WITH SOLVENT-BASED INK. NEXT, BRUSH RESIST MEDIUM ONTO LETTER STAMP AND STAMP OVER THE CIRCLES. ALLOW TO DRY. [2] BRUSH A THIN LAYER OF WHITE PAINT OVER THE WHOLE STRIP AND ALLOW TO DRY. [3] RUN THE STRIP UNDER WARM WATER. AGITATE SLIGHTLY WITH FINGERS UNTIL THE RESIST MEDIUM BREAKS AWAY. ALLOW TO DRY. IRON IF NECESSARY.

WILLY WONKA

JESSIE BALDWIN
LAS VEGAS, NEVADA

A wacky, wild part in a school play called for a layout just as fun, which Jessie accomplished here on this crazy, commemorative piece. Colorful circle and star stickers create a fun-fueled feeling and source of movement about the page, eliciting the same whimsical attitude found in the story. For authenticity, Jessie tucked the Willy Wonka play program behind her focal photo.

Supplies: Sticker shapes (Creative Imaginations); stamps (Technique Tuesday); solvent ink; acrylic paint; pen; cardstock; Willy Wonka play program

ON YOUR MARK, GET SET, BLOW

VANESSA HUDSON
MT. OLIVE, ALABAMA

Sporting her favorite colors and essential scrapbook supplies, Savannah's paper car project may not have been the fastest in her class but was definitely the cutest! Vanessa applauds her daughter's automotive innovation here on this fun and feminine layout. She pieced together her background with angled strips of peppy and preppy patterns, inking the edges with coordinating pink for emphasis. Sanded edges around her chipboard letters give Vanessa's title bold definition, while a funky flower adorning a playful button adds a burst of whimsy.

Supplies: Patterned paper (Bo-Bunny Press); chipboard letters (Pressed Petals); button, flower (Doodlebug Designs); photo turns (Sizzix); dye ink; cardstock

One of the incentives given to the children at Jefferson School to sell more magazines during their school fundraiser was the promise of a crazy hair day. And as is obvious from these pictures, that goal was met, and the kids embraced their opportunity to go a 'little crazy.'

Camron interpreted crazy hair day as an opportunity to be a thug for a day. With slicked back hair and a hooded sweatshirt, he appears like the gangsters he idolizes on MTV.

Cam's friend, Ryan, shocked us with a red and blue spiked fro. With his long, thick hair, it was quite a sight.

CRAZY HAIR DAY

AMBER BALEY
WAUPUN, WISCONSIN

The only thing that could be more fun than a crazy hair day at school was the opportunity for Amber to create an uninhibited page design commemorating her son's event. Amber arranged cut paper strips and tied ribbon at angles to frame her focal-point photo. Machine zig-zag stitching around and through her images and accents adds to the wild attitude of the page, while providing texture and subtle balance among the angled strips. The most fun for Amber was dying her chipboard title letters by hand, dipping them into boiled water with acrylic paint added. She dipped the letters three times, drying in a 250° F (121° C) heated oven between coats, with a finishing coat of diamond glaze completing the look.

Supplies: Patterned paper (7 Gypsies, Chatterbox); chipboard letters (Li'l Davis Designs, Making Memories); tag (Making Memories); vellum (Grafix); fabric tag (Me & My Big Ideas); ribbon (Chatterbox); dimensional glaze; key ring; thread; Handwritten, Weather Fence fonts (Two Peas in a Bucket)

HAVING A FIELD DAY

BARB PFEFFER
OMAHA, NEBRASKA

The proverbial field day springs to life on Barbara's lively layout, embracing her daughter's most eagerly anticipated school year tradition. The photo collage, incorporating a playful patterned paper strip and journaling block as well, captures highlights from Field Day and her daughter in action, perfectly illustrating the pink printed details. Barbara kept the design simple, rounding the corners of her collage to play well with the polka dot print, and adding die-cut arrows for movement and flow.

Supplies: Patterned paper, rub-ons (Scrapworks); chipboard letters (Heidi Swapp); die-cuts (QuicKutz); corner rounder; cardstock

HAVING A field day

As active as you are, it's no surprise that Field Day is one of your most eagerly anticipated traditions of the school year. This year, your favorite events were the sponge relay, where team members must fill a bucket of water one sponge-full at a time; the tandem "cross country skiing" event, where teams of 4 "ski" across the grass on boards with rope handles, and the traditional tug of war (the girls won, yay!). You didn't much care for the long distance run though. You were beginning to wilt in the heat and sun, so you alternated between walking and jogging. But a popsicle from the break stand perked you right back up for the next set of events. All in all, you had the proverbial field day!

PLAY IS GOOD

PHOTO CHECKLIST

★ Homework routines
★ Back-to-school shopping
★ Handwritten daily schedule
★ Character growth
★ Involvement in the Arts
★ Back-to-school family traditions
★ Sports activities
★ Field trips
★ Favorite class projects
★ First crushes
★ School plays
★ Theme days at school

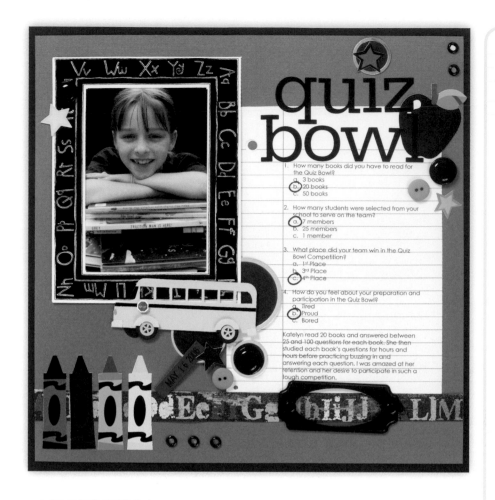

QUIZ BOWL

JENNIFER GALLACHER
AMERICAN FORK, UTAH

Jennifer's favorite student shines on this design dedicated to her daughter's drive for academic excellence. The event commemorated, a multi-school quiz challenge, served as the inspiration for the journaling section, which Jennifer printed in a quiz format. She circled the correct statistics with red pen, for the look of a teacher's markings, and then had tons of fun embellishing the remainder of the page with school supply stickers and die cuts. The alphabet frame balances the weight of the alphabet paper strip along the bottom.

Supplies: Patterned paper (Bo-Bunny Press, Karen Foster Design); letter stickers (American Crafts); alphabet frame (My Mind's Eye); accent stickers (Pebbles); tags, eyelets (Making Memories); die-cut bus (Jolee's Boutique); bookplate (Creative Imaginations); buttons (source unknown); cardstock

GRANDPARENTS DAY

BARB HOGAN
CINCINNATI, OHIO

As Shannon embraced the opportunity to bring her grandparents to school with her, Barb celebrated the fun on this stellar combination of sentiment and play. By cutting a wave design into her corner sections of patterned paper, Barb provides a well-balanced sense of movement and flow, contradicting the graphic lines and angles of the central star shape. Using a template, Barb assembled the star with patterned paper pieces and a central photo. A ribbon tied in the upper right corner gives a sweet linear look juxtaposing hand-doodled swirls and dots.

Supplies: Patterned paper (A2Z Essentials); chipboard letters (Imagination Project); ribbon (Michaels); stickers (SEI); pigment ink; pen; cardstock

FIELD TRIP

KIM KESTI
PHOENIX, ARIZONA

Americana abounds on Kim's all star salute to local firefighters and her daughter's class trip to a firefighter festival. Wanting to incorporate a large number of photos without overwhelming the page design, Kim established a smaller photo border at the bottom and kept her focal-point photo in full 4" x 6" (10cm x 15cm) format. A handful of buttons along the edge of her journaling block, fabric title letters, a few patriotic woven tabs and patterned paper strips were all that were needed to enliven the look with texture and dimension.

Supplies: Patterned paper, tabs, border, fabric letters (Scrapworks); envelope (Bazzill); buttons (Doodlebug Designs); cardstock; Arial font (Microsoft)

A moment lasts all of a second,

field trip

Miss Erickson's class was lucky enough to be able to attend the 2006 Fireman's Muster in downtown Phoenix. And, I was lucky enough to be asked to chaperon. It was an exciting day filled with exhibits, demonstrations, games and contests. Sophie and her classmates enjoyed every bit of it. But, her very favorite part was getting a turn to hold the big fire hose. She was really impressed with how far that water flew! Maybe she'll become a fireman, um, firewoman someday!

THE DIFFERENCE A SCHOOL YEAR MAKES

CAROLINE HUOT
LAVAL, QUEBEC, CANADA

The wild transformation of a new fifth grader into a ready-for-sixth grader evolves before your very eyes here on Caroline's comical comparison of her son's first and last day of his school year. She kept the layout simple, allowing the two photos matted on patterned paper to speak volumes on their own. Using epoxy stencil-type letters, Caroline created her title, which adds visual weight to the bottom of the page.

Supplies: Patterned paper (BasicGrey, DDDesigns7); letters stickers (Li'l Davis Designs); rub-ons (Bobarbo); labels (Acme); brads; pigment ink; cardstock

- Your backpack's handle is broken
- Your backpack has been stitched up several times
- Your lunchbox is good for the garbage now
- Your shoes have deteriorated beyond belief (but yet it's impressive that they still fit!)
- Your hair has grown quite long: the "in" look
- You've grown several centimetres
- You've gained so much new knowledge
- You're ready for 6th grade & English immersion

THE DIFFERENCE a school year makes

AUGUST 2005
MAY 2006

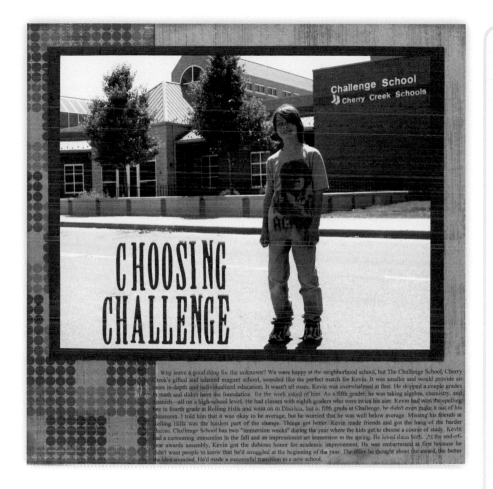

CHOOSING CHALLENGE

KELLI NOTO
CENTENNIAL, COLORADO

A new school means major changes, as Kelli details on this layout describing her son's move to a more advanced learning experience. The single large photo packs a bold punch on the page and a sense of overcoming the challenges that come with testing one's own capabilities. Kelli adhered her die cut title letters directly onto the photo, filling the negative space in the image. Her journaling was printed onto clear self-adhesive computer paper, allowing the subtle pattern of her background paper to shine through.

Supplies: Patterned paper (Adorn It); die-cut letters (QuickKutz); self-adhesive clear computer paper (ChartPak); chalk ink

CROSSROADS

BARB PFEFFER
OMAHA, NEBRASKA

A parent's dilemma for knowing what is best for her child's education is expressed here on Barbara's compassionate creation, acknowledging her daughter's disappointment with her decision for schools. The single photo captures the heart of the page and shared emotion, while decorative rub-on embellishments accentuated with rhinestones draw out the beauty of the situation enveloped in a mother's prayerful wisdom.

Supplies: Patterned paper (BasicGrey); rub-ons (BasicGrey, K & Company); letter stickers (Making Memories); rhinestones (K & Company); cardstock; Papyrus font (Internet download)

MY GRADUATE

VANESSA HUDSON
MT. OLIVE, ALABAMA

Cheerful exuberance meets sophisticated style here on Vanessa's milestone memory page dedicated to her daughter's school year graduation. Vanessa stitched blocks of festive patterned papers together, embellished with classy floral rub-ons. She gave ownership to pre-printed chipboard rounds by adding decorative coordinating rub-ons overtop. The black chipboard letters and black cardstock background set a formal tone for the layout and emphasize the theme of graduation.

Supplies: Patterned paper, chipboard circles (Imagination Project); chipboard letters (Heidi Swapp); rub-ons (BasicGrey); photo turn (7 Gypsies); brads; thread; cardstock

MINI ALBUM – ALL ABOUT YOU

CHRISTINE TRAVERSA
JOLIET, ILLINOIS

Christine wanted to create a keepsake that her daughter would cherish for years to come. Blessed with a comedic genius, her little actress-in-training had so many amazing experiences during her 2006 school year that a mini album proved to be the perfect format for telling her story. Christine began by covering the outside of the album with patterned paper, floral trim, ribbon and a paper flower. The inside holds additional decorative elements including stickers, handwritten journaling and photographs. Each page shares a different adventure that keeps the viewer wondering what life holds next for this talented young lady.

Supplies: Chipboard album (Maya Road); patterned paper, stickers, ribbon, trim (Making Memories); flower (Prima); label (Dymo); decorative trimmer (Creative Memories); image editing software (Adobe); rubber stamp (Penny Black); solvent ink; pen

MINI ALBUMS

Take your creativity a step further by expanding your pages into mini albums, each covering a single topic about your star pupil. The album format will provide additional real estate for photos, memorabilia and journaling. You can choose to create an album about an event or accomplishment during a single school year, or create a theme-based album that you add to each year. The options are endless! Here are some ideas to get you started.

★ Field trips or class outings to museums, zoos, aquariums, etc.
★ Favorite books or authors
★ Academic achievements
★ Scouting, camping or group outdoor activities
★ Arts and crafts or other creative projects
★ Playing musical instruments, singing or acting
★ Class parties or special events
★ End-of-the-year school activities
★ Graduation

TRY

TRY

AGAIN

As the summer drew to a close it was time for Jim to think about the new school year ahead. He was in for some major changes with moving up to the Middle School and I was gearing myself up as well to help him deal with the big changes a new school would bring. Things like:

- Learning a new schedule with nine classroom changes and nine new teachers.
- Moving from a class of 100 fifth graders to a class of 800 sixth graders.
- Finding his way in an unfamiliar building with an additional 800 Middle School savvy seventh graders.
- Tackling harder subjects.
- Making new friends.
- Operating a locker with a ... gulp ... combination lock and only three minutes between classes!

Yes — the dreaded combination locker predicament - the bane of every new sixth grader's existence. It seems that the goal of every soon-to-be seventh grader is to instill a dizzying fear of combination lock mastery into every incoming sixth grader they meet. And so in the days before the start of school Jim practiced time and time again. Spinning the dial while I encouraged from the sidelines while chanting the mantra, "If at first you don't succeed, try try again." And as he walked through the door after the first day of school, I held my breath as I asked the dreaded question ... "How did it go with the locker?" to which he replied, "Piece-a-cake!"

September, 2005

If at first you don't succeed, try, try, again. If at first you don't succeed, try, try, again. If at first you don't succeed, try, try, again. If at first you don't succeed, try, try, again.

Master

CHAPTER 3

SAVED BY THE BELL

[Grades 6 – 8]

Turn around, your child has a blankie and Show-and-Tell; turn around, your child has school plays and best friends; turn around, your child has braces and acne—Middle School has arrived! While some parents fear it and other parents embrace it for what it is, the Middle School years are a time of wonder to be documented for sure. Welcome to the awkward years of disproportionate bodies, squeaking voices and hair not-to dos! With more changes happening in your child than in his or her wardrobe before the bus arrives, pre-adolescence marks rapid growth in all areas of your child's life. Treasure this tender and tumultuous ride of enjoying the emerging young adult in your child, while encouraging the part of him or her that still loves just simply being a kid. Celebrate first dances, identity-seeking trends, growth spurts and technology know-how on scrapbook pages both you and your child will love and laugh at in years to come.

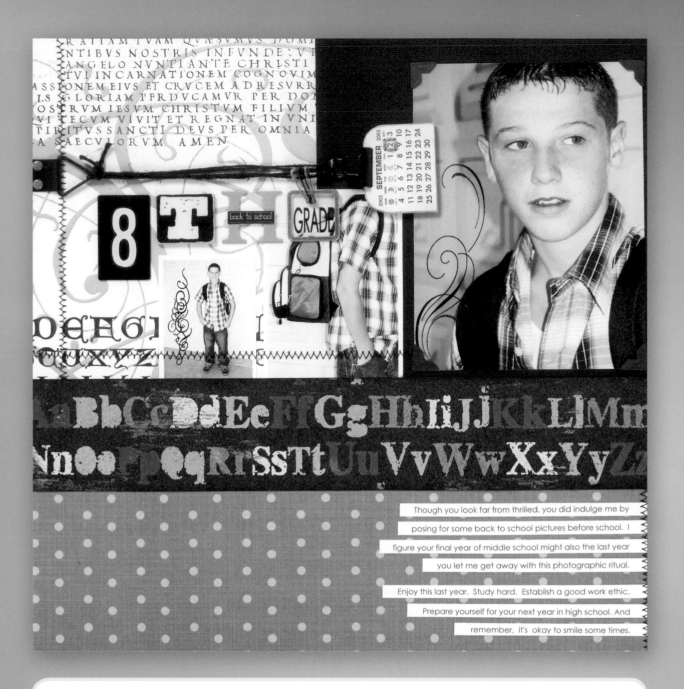

Though you look far from thrilled, you did indulge me by posing for some back to school pictures before school. I figure your final year of middle school might also the last year you let me get away with this photographic ritual.

Enjoy this last year. Study hard. Establish a good work ethic. Prepare yourself for your next year in high school. And remember, it's okay to smile some times.

8TH GRADE

AMBER BALEY
WAUPUN, WISCONSIN

While her son may have been somewhat reluctant to smile for first-day photos of his last year of junior high, Amber managed to capture a few images that showcase the cool factor of eighth grade. She created her own chipboard calendar accent by cutting chipboard to size with her calendar page and then rounding the tops of both, for the appearance of a clipboard. After adhering the calendar to the chipboard, she sanded the edges for a gritty, masculine edge, then hand stitched around the date for texture.

Supplies: Patterned paper (7 Gypsies, Bo-Bunny Press, Chatterbox); chipboard letters (Li'l Davis Designs, Making Memories); number, tag (Making Memories); photo hanger (Daisy D's); brads; safety pins (Queen & Co.); stickers (7 Gypsies); rub-ons (BasicGrey); solvent ink; calendar, twine, clip, embroidery floss; cardstock

EXPLORE

JENNIFER GALLACHER
AMERICAN FORK, UTAH

New beginnings are celebrated here on Jennifer's earth-toned tribute to her son's rite of passage into junior high. Jennifer chose patterned papers reminiscent of school projects, such as map themes, script prints and geometric shapes, along with squares of cork, to create her quilt-style collage grid. Her dynamic title block on the left poses as a powerful page element on its own, made up of simple letter stickers, with coordinating patterned paper set behind several letters to unify the overall design. Tan photo corners in the upper and lower left establish boundaries and tie the composition together.

Supplies: Patterned paper (BasicGrey, Karen Foster Design); letter stickers (Target); tab (Autumn Leaves); star buttons (source unknown); round buttons (Making Memories); wooden letters (Li'l Davis Designs); date stamp (Staples); stamping ink; photo turn (7 Gypsies); brad; photo corners; cardstock

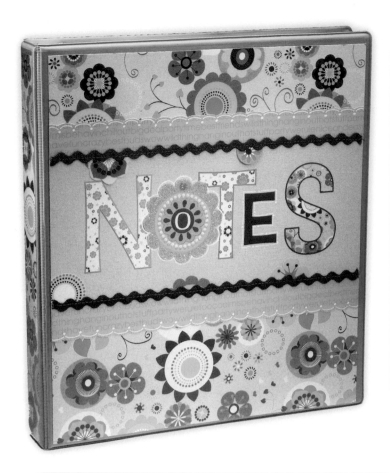

NOTES

VANESSA HUDSON
MT. OLIVE, ALABAMA

School supplies may come a dime a dozen, but what girl wouldn't love a handmade touch to make her notebook stand out above the rest? Vanessa took her daughter's ordinary binder from drab to fab with a garden of patterned papers, pink rickrack, a glitter sticker and fanciful rub-on letters. A white gel pen adds the perfect finishing touch to this unique school day treasure that was a snap to put together.

Supplies: Binder (Avery); patterned paper, rub-ons, stickers (Me & My Big Ideas); rickrack (May Arts); pen; cardstock

BOOKS

ANGIE HEAD
FRIENDSWOOD, TEXAS

The love of learning is a shared passion in Caleb's family, as Angie illustrates on her literary creation, celebrating one of the major highlights of beginning seventh grade as a homeschooling family. Angie arranged the new collection of books in an interesting arrangement, and took the focal-point photo from a unique perspective. She printed out Caleb's booklist for the year onto coordinating cardstock and set it as a backdrop for her photos and journaling. Sanded edges on her photos add a well-loved, timeless touch to the page, meshing with the vintage patterned papers in her title letter creations.

Supplies: Patterned paper (Crate Paper, Design Originals, Karen Foster Design, Making Memories); rub-ons (Creative Imaginations); tag (7 Gypsies); brad; twill (Autumn Leaves); chalk ink; solvent ink; pen; cardstock

BACK TO SCHOOL SHOPPING

KELLI NOTO
CENTENNIAL, COLORADO

Eric gets his fash-on with a little help from his style emergency experts, Alison and Amy, who were more than willing to assist with his back-to-school shopping. Kelli captured the exciting energy of the event on this bold and bright page modeling all that's fresh and funky. A die-cut checkmark on the focal-point image shows the thrill of creating a fashion find, while the accent image with a die-cut negative lends humor to the page by showcasing a definite fashion faux pas. A black cardstock background and matting give this page its dynamic intensity, while inked die-cut accents add emphasis as well.

Supplies: Patterned paper (Flair Designs); die cut letters and shapes (QuickKutz); foam spacers; cardstock

JOURNALING

Shake it up by trying new journaling techniques. There's a wealth of possibilities for conveying the events and happenings of your child's school year both visually and through words. Try these fun journaling options to jazz up your school-days pages.

★ Calendars and timelines
★ Interviews between parent and child and/or teacher and child
★ List of child's favorite items or school subjects
★ Journaling written from child's perspective
★ Journaling written as a comic strip
★ Journaling written as a fairy tale
★ Inclusion of personal letter to child or personal letter from child
★ Step-by-step journaling

Back To School Shopping

Eric lacks an innate fashion sense and his mom is just a little too old to be of help when it comes to what's hip with the teen crowd. Luckily for Eric, Alison and Amy were willing to go back-to-school shopping with him. The girls would pull clothes off the rack and have Eric try them on. They'd issue either a thumbs up or down and the clothes would go into the pile of things to purchase or back to the racks. In just over an hour, Eric had a closet full of new clothes and my credit card had seen significant use. When a couple of cute girls on the cutting edge of cool tell your son what clothes to buy, the only thing a mom can do is open up her wallet. All three kids had a great time shopping and they keep asking when we can do it again.

Outfit for the first day of school: $100

Cost of a public school education:

Accessories: *classified*

SCHOOL BUS

School supplies: $150

FREE

thank goodness - because I'm broke!

THE COST OF EDUCATION

KITTY FOSTER
SNELLVILLE, GEORGIA

Kitty takes a light-hearted look at back to school expenses on her sassy and stylish creation, which celebrates the joy of the free public school education. Utilizing the complementary red and green color scheme from the photos, Kitty coordinates the page with striped background paper offset with stylish sticker strips. A cheerful patterned arrow serves as a fashionable accent on the page, while pulling the eye down to the humorous journaling. The sanded chipboard letters carry out the punch-line with a look of distress.

Supplies: Patterned paper, stickers (Bo-Bunny Press); chipboard letters (Pressed Petals); dye ink; black beads (source unknown); cardstock

TRY, TRY AGAIN

LISA DIXON
EAST BRUNSWICK, NEW JERSEY

"The dreaded combination locker predicament," as Lisa describes it, is the focus of her layout, featuring her son's biggest first-day-of-sixth-grade fear. The black-and-white photos coordinate with the locker paper and lock element and create a steely-nerved effect against distressed patterned paper. The lock embellishment was created by enlarging an image of a lock to 5" x 7" (13cm x 18cm), printing out three copies. Using computer software, Lisa formed her quote into a circle, copying and pasting the circle shape twice in reduced sizes, randomly rotated. She printed out two copies of the quote arrangement onto vellum, which she then cut into a circle and layered over the three layered photos. Foam adhesive spacers adhere the layers together with dimension.

Supplies: Patterned paper (Crate Paper, Karen Foster Design); vellum (Paper Adventure); ribbon (Offray); distress ink; pen; cardstock; Arial Black, Tahoma fonts (Microsoft)

As the summer drew to a close it was time for Jim to think about the new school year ahead. He was in for some major changes with moving up to the Middle School and I was gearing myself up as well to help him deal with the big changes a new school would bring. Things like:

- Learning a new schedule with nine classroom changes and nine new teachers.
- Moving from a class of 100 fifth graders to a class of 800 sixth graders.
- Finding his way in an unfamiliar building with an additional 800 Middle School savvy seventh graders.
- Tackling harder subjects.
- Making new friends.
- Operating a locker with a ... gulp ... combination lock and only three minutes between classes!

Yes – the dreaded combination locker predicament - the bane of every new sixth grader's existence. It seems that the goal of every soon-to-be seventh grader is to instill a dizzying fear of combination lock mastery into every incoming sixth grader they meet. And so in the days before the start of school Jim practiced time and time again. Spinning the dial while I encouraged from the sidelines while chanting the mantra, "If at first you don't succeed, try, try again." And as he walked through the door after the first day of school, I held my breath as I asked the dreaded question ... "How did it go with the locker?" to which he replied, "Piece-a-cake!"

September, 2005

Wednesdays mean study group. This time each week affords you the opportunity to complete various assignments alongside fellow students that are studying the same subject matter as you are. Working together as a team teaches all of you not only the academics of your studies but it builds camaraderie and it helps each of you to appreciate thoughts and opinions other than your own. Here, you and Sean are working together to complete a map of Alexander the Great's conquests. As usual, the two of you will work diligently and briskly through the assignment in order to be the first one's finished with all of the answer's correct. Both of you are good students with a hint of overachiever mixed in there! Spring 2006

STUDY GROUP

ANGIE HEAD
FRIENDSWOOD, TEXAS

Hard at work, this dynamic duo hits the books together in their weekly study group, which Angie showcases on this bright and boisterous design. While the patterns may appear complex, she kept the composition simple, layering patterned papers in coordinating color palettes and prints. After mounting her photo onto patterned paper, she tipped the left upper corner down for visual interest and added a coordinating trio of brads. Angie repeated the colorful brad arrangement in two other sets around the image.

Supplies: Patterned papers (Crossed Paths); brads (Bazzill), chipboard letters, acrylic paint (Making Memories); chalk ink; cardstock; CAC One Seventy font (Internet download)

SHE'S GOT CLASS

**SHARON LAAKKONEN
SUPERIOR, WISCONSIN**

Not only does Sharon have these beautiful keepsake images of her daughter to light up her layout, but her daughter's reflections on each of her eighth grade classes is commemorated here as well, in her own words and writing. The simple arrangement of blue cardstock overtop playful patterned paper is set on its edge by angling her photo arrangement. Paper flower embellishments give the page delicate dazzle with shimmering beads added to each center. Sharon coordinated the beads with the patterned paper and set decorative brads over each notebook paper journaling strip to complete the look.

Supplies: Patterned paper (Provo Craft); chipboard letters, rub-ons (Imaginations Project); flowers (Prima); beads, brads (Queen & Co.); stamping ink; notebook paper; pen; embroidery floss; cardstock

Your Homework is on *THAT* little thing??

Kevin does his assignments on the laptop and then carries his homework to school in a tiny jump drive. He uses the internet for research and creates Powerpoint presentations instead of poster boards.

Another advantage of technology is the ability of parents to log online and see the teachers' gradebooks (much to the students chagrin).

There are advantages to having technologically-advanced kids. I can always count on them to install a new printer for me or have them help me figure out how to type text in the shapes of a circle.

JUMPDRIVE

KELLI NOTO
CENTENNIAL, COLORADO

Celebrating all things digital on this traditional paper design, Kelli used a large single photo to showcase the way her son transports homework from school to his home laptop on a tiny jump drive. The remainder of the page was kept simple, using only two small blocks of patterned paper overtop her layered, chalk-inked solid background. Energy abounds from the bouncing border journaling along the bottom, where Kelli shares her thoughts on technology at school. She printed her journaling to fit into the circle shape, and then set several on foam adhesive spacers for depth and visual interest.

Supplies: Patterned paper (Imagination Project); chalk ink; self-adhesive clear computer paper (ChartPak); circle cutter; foam spacers; cardstock

LOCKER CLIPBOARD

CHRISTINE TRAVERSA
JOLIET, ILLINOIS

In the action-packed world of middle school education, a girl's locker is the one place she can call her own. Christine put her collection of scrapbook supplies to good use in creating this hip-and-happening locker clipboard with accompanying notebook and pencil. She inked the pre-covered clipboard for definition and added a mixture of girly accents to the notebook and metal clip. Rub-on flowers and butterflies add a dash of delight while rhinestones, chipboard accents and ribbon add a fanciful flair.

Supplies: Pre-covered clipboard, patterned pencil (Tri Coastal Design); chipboard (Autumn Leaves); ribbon (American Crafts, Michaels); rub-ons (Fancy Pants Designs, Imagination Project); jewels (Darice); ribbon holder (Maya Road); solvent ink; staples

life is good.

smile

VANITY AFTERMATH

KITTY FOSTER
SNELLVILLE, GEORGIA

The aftermath of a teenager's fashion preparations for school are highlighted here on Kitty's whimsical and wise page creation. The stylish design was established by cutting the circle edged border along the khaki cardstock and then inking the edges. She then set a lively and fashionable look overtop by adhering patterned paper circles, punched from a variety of papers, with edges inked for drama. Bountiful buttons and thematic purse and footwear embellishments polish off the page with a spirit of style.

Supplies: Patterned paper (My Mind's Eye); buttons (Junkitz); accessory accents (Target); circle punch; chalk ink; cardstock; International, Lighthouse fonts (Two Peas in a Bucket)

Should getting ready for school really be this hard? This is your closet after only one morning of clothing indecision. The sooner you learn that you are what make the outfit, the easier your life will be and I will continue to pray for patience.

OUT OF THIS WORLD

JENNIFER GALLACHER
AMERICAN FORK, UTAH

Jennifer's galactic masterpiece beams with a mother's pride over her son's science project, modeled to precision by himself. Deep celestial blues align with light, airy greens to create a masculine, yet youthful energy on the page, while extreme patterns and cosmic embellishments play up the theme of the solar system. Jennifer formed the lower left accent by mounting the clipboard elements onto the layout, and then layering the star die-cuts and metal label holder overtop. Large black eyelets set along the bottom finish off the page with a bold border, while repeating the circular pattern of the papers and emphasized title.

Supplies: Patterned paper (American Crafts, Daisy D's, Deja Views, Making Memories, Scenic Route Paper Co.); letter stickers (KI Memories); star die-cuts (My Mind's Eye); eyelets (Making Memories); chipboard stars (Li'l Davis Designs); clipboards (Provo Craft); bookplate, photo corners (Creative Imaginations); cardstock

WORK 2 PLAY

DENISE TUCKER
VERSAILLES, INDIANA

All work and no playing throughout the school-week make Tanner one straight-A student, indeed, as his mother attests on this layout featuring her son's true weekend motivator: X Box 360! School-themed papers set the tone for Denise's design, while time-clock paper scanned and printed onto peach cardstock serves as the perfect place for printed journaling. Denise enhanced the look of the page with teen spirit by printing the round X-Box logo onto white cardstock, while the written logo was printed onto transparency and heat embossed, along with the key ring, then adhered to white chipboard. For final fun, Denise placed a letter and 3-D number sticker into bottle caps, which she filled with decoupage medium.

Supplies: Patterned paper, chipboard letters (Rusty Pickle); transparency; paper protector (Krylon); rivets (Chatterbox); bottle caps (Design Originals); number (Colorbok); letter sticker (Memories Complete); embossing powder; acrylic paint; decoupage medium; die (EK Success); stamping ink; distress ink, foam squares; brand logo (Internet download); brand keychain (Microsoft)

GEARING UP

BARB HOGAN
CINCINNATI, OHIO

A classic, tailored look on Barb's design draws upon the personal style and personality of this featured middle schooler, prepping for school. Barb's unique photographs step the viewer through this student's daily process of getting ready for school, from fixing hair to applying makeup, to landing at the final destination of a seat on the bus. Deep, rich colors lend festive sophistication to the page, while winsome patterns and movement through brads and trim lend dimension and adolescent charm.

Supplies: Patterned paper (Chatterbox, Paper Loft); letter stickers (Karen Foster Design); brads (source unknown); rickrack (Coordinates Collections); labels (source unknown); cardstock

BOOK COVER & BOOKMARK

LISA DIXON
EAST BRUNSWICK, NEW JERSEY

To help her son keep his reading supplies organized in one handy spot, Lisa turned a traditional composition notebook into a decorative journal complete with pencil, sticky notes and bookmark. She covered the front of the journal with patterned papers reflecting the literature theme. Ruler and letter stickers along with a matchbox-style note holder provide further embellishment. A traditional check out library card serves double duty as a bookmark and a place to record a list of must-read books.

Supplies: Composition notebook; patterned paper, letter stickers, tag stickers (Carson-Dellosa); rub-ons (Making Memories); library card and holder (Boxer Productions); barbed elastic (7 Gypsies); distress ink; sticky notepad; self-adhesive magnet strip; pencil; cardstock

WEIGHTLIFTING 101

LISA DIXON
EAST BRUNSWICK, NEW JERSEY

It's double duty for Lisa's son, who requires two backpacks to lug around all of his books from class-to-class, due to his overcrowded middle school locker rules. Lisa used primitive looking patterns for her background to play up the barbarian image of her son in the focal photo, and enhanced the look with a coordinating shape cut from chipboard, and then distressed with inks and sandpaper. Acrylic paint was applied to the large chipboard monogram on the left to further the rustic effect, while two backpack accessories balance out the page with polished thematic pizzazz.

Supplies. Patterned paper (BasicGrey); letter stickers (Chatterbox); chipboard monogram (Rusty Pickle); ribbon (Making Memories); metal tag (7 Gypsies); rubber stamps (Hero Arts); backpack sticker (EK Success); acrylic paints; chipboard; waxed linen thread; distress ink; cardstock

If only Jim could earn school credits for lifting his backpack; he'd be assured of at least one A+ on his report card. Each year just when I think these blasted backpacks couldn't possibly get any heavier, somehow the school manages to prove me wrong. And sixth graders have it the worst! With English, Science, Social Studies, Foreign Language, Mathematics, Study Hall and the Cycle classes, there's enough textbooks, workbooks, folders, binders and packets to make King Kong's knees buckle! Poor Jim – one backpack just couldn't handle the job of holding it all so he's stuck with lugging around two every single day. Who needs to pump iron when you've got 30 pounds of schoolbooks to carry!

CLASS PICNIC

BARB HOGAN
CINCINNATI, OHIO

The day before school lets out for the summer means class picnic time for Barb's favorite middle schooler! Barb used a single manufacturer's collection of patterned papers and cardstock stickers to create this lively and lighthearted layout, removing all the stress of coordinating papers and elements. Festive flowers at the bottom of the page were formed from cardstock stickers and rick-rack, while carefree ribbons stapled to the title block carry on the whimsical feel and create a pennant-like effect.

Supplies: Patterned paper, stickers (Arctic Frog); ribbon (May Arts, Offray); brads (Scrapworks); staples; rickrack; circle punch; cardstock; Hot Chocolate font (Two Peas in a Bucket)

PHOTO CHECKLIST

* ★ Favorite fashions and trends
* ★ Coursework commentary
* ★ Physical and character traits
* ★ Then and now comparisons
* ★ Involvement in the Arts
* ★ School prepping and primping rituals
* ★ Awards received and special honors
* ★ Social involvements and extracurricular activities
* ★ Untraditional schooling methods
* ★ New school buildings
* ★ Technology at school
* ★ First dances

Ethan was totally amazing this year in band class. I don't think he had ever even read a musical note before starting class. He borrowed Uncle Russell's trumpet and showed up ready to work. Not only did he learn his notes, some music theory and even history, he actually learned how to play! It wasn't work, it was fun!

celebrate

PALO VERDE
MIDDLE SCHOOL
2005 - 2006

Most Improved

Ethan Kesti

my son

What started out as a lark (he planned to quit after one year) has turned into quite the musical adventure. Ethan was even honored at the end of the year as Most Improved Student! He was so proud, and we were, too!

CELEBRATE

KIM KESTI
PHOENIX, ARIZONA

Wanting to celebrate her son's well-deserved music award as "Most Improved" musician, Kim created this festive design to commemorate the occasion. Cardstock arrows draw emphasis to the images of Ethan's trumpet, his award and the band at play, while patterned paper strips threaded through each arrow further the movement and energy of the page. She pulled the varying photos together with a simple wooden token set in the middle.

Supplies: Patterned paper (A2Z Essentials); arrows, coaster (Imagination Project); acrylic paint; stamping ink; wooden token (Sweetwater Designs); rub-on (Scenic Route Paper Co.); pen; cardstock

2ND CHAIR

KELLI NOTO
CENTENNIAL, COLORADO

The beauty of being second chair in the eighth grade band is summed up succinctly on Kelli's dark and dreamy visual ballad to her son. Kelli used an 8" x 12" (20cm x 30cm) photo to fill the bulk of the page and to capture the sentimental emotion of her son embracing his musical gifts with a humble attitude. She set her accent image on foam adhesive spacers for dramatic impact, and surrounded it with grunge-effect rub-on letters for boyish charm. By overlapping her title and journaling, Kelli ties the composition of the page together, creating a smooth-flowing groove.

Supplies: Cardstock; die-cut letters and shapes (QuicKutz); rub-on letters (Creative Imaginations); clear self-adhesive computer paper (ChartPak); foam spacers

2nd Chair

It is good being second chair. There is a comfort in knowing that you aren't expected to be the best, but you are still high enough to be thought of as good. There are constant challenges from the folks who are wanting to move up a chair. Mr. Ehrle gives us a piece of music that we are expected to play sight unseen and whoever makes the fewest mistakes wins the challenge. I have never challenged the first chair, never wanted to move up, and never wanted the pressure of performing a solo in concert.

Trumpet

8th Grade Band

the **UN**
Club

X Outdoors Club
X Drama Club
X Choir
X Math Club
X Orchestra

If it weren't for UNclub, there'd be no club at all!

Hannah, I tried & tried to encourage you to join a club this year. I thought it would help you find your niche and as a typical teenager, you had other plans. There was no way you were going to join any club just for the sake of fitting in – not a chance! I know that finding out who you are is will never come from a club, it comes from within. Regardless of what you choose, you will succeed - - and that is no

X **UN**derstatment!

THE UNCLUB

KITTY FOSTER
SNELLVILLE, GEORGIA

Since her daughter chose *not* to be involved with extra curricular clubs at school, Kitty designed this lighthearted page around her daughter's social un-involvement! Kitty chose a red, white and black color scheme, cutting around the top and bottom edges of her polka-dot paper for fun. She mounted her daughter's black-and-white image onto red script paper, accentuated with black script photo corners. After printing her journaling onto a cut piece of 6½" x 10" (17cm x 25cm) cardstock, Kitty adhered her matted photo overtop. Additional text was printed on file folder labels and adhered to the page. The labels were embellished with strips of black cardstock to form the "X's."

Supplies: Patterned paper, rub-ons (Creative Imaginations); chipboard letters (Pressed Petals); white labels (Avery); chalk ink; cardstock; Times New Roman font (Microsoft)

AMONGST YOUR PEERS

AMBER BALEY
WAUPUN, WISCONSIN

Despite a late-season injury, Amber's son showed his loyalty to his football team by continuing to attend practices and games, which Amber applauds here on this celebratory layout. Using the computer, she created her title and digital frame directly on her photo before printing them out, and then stitched her photo/journaling corners by hand. Although her background paper is trimmed to create an overall 12" x 12" layout, her star embellishment, cut from patterned paper and mounted on cardstock, hangs slightly off the edge of the page. Strips of patterned paper form the shooting star effect, which Amber enhanced with rub-on stitches.

Supplies: Patterned paper (K & Company); rub-ons (Die Cuts With A View); index tab (7 Gypsies); brads (Queen & Co.); digital frame (Jessica Sprague); embroidery floss; cardstock

AMONGST YOUR **PEERS**

FOOTBALL THIS YEAR WAS YOUR FIRST TIME PLAYING FOR YOUR SCHOOL INSTEAD OF COMMUNITY SPORTS.

IT WAS DIFFICULT AT THE BEGINNING OF THE SEASON. STARTING OUT IN 8TH GRADE, YOU WERE A BIT OF A LATE COMER— YOUR CLASSMATES HAD ALREADY ESTABLISHED THEIR POSITION ON THE TEAM THE PREVIOUS TWO YEARS AND YOU DIDN'T GET THE SPOT YOU WANTED. YOU WERE FRUSTRATED AND TALKED ABOUT QUITTING, BUT YOU STUCK IT OUT, AND I'M PROUD OF YOU FOR STAYING WITH IT. WHEN YOUR COACH REALIZED YOUR ABILITY AND PLACED YOU IN THE DEFENSIVE TACKLE POSITION, YOU FOUND YOUR GROOVE.

YOU WERE INJURED LATE IN THE SEASON, BUT YOU SURPRISED US BY STILL ATTENDING PRACTICES AND GAMES, EVEN THOUGH YOU HAD TO WATCH FROM THE SIDELINES. IT WAS UNLIKE YOU. SCHOOL SPORTS HAD AN IMPACT ON YOU. PLAYING AMONGST YOUR PEERS HAD A POSITIVE INFLUENCE THAT I HOPE YOU TAKE WITH YOU.

PULL

PULL

How Cool Were You?
Levi's rolled up
Daddy's old High School Letter Jacket
Fresh White T-shirt with the sleeves rolled up
Brand Spankin' New Black Converse {Chuck's}
That look on your face
PACES Classical School Annual Fundraiser 'Sock Hop'

50 years
too late

paces SOCK HOP

CREATE A VINTAGE RECORD

[1] GATHER AN OLD CD OR SPACER, ADHESIVE, DIMENSIONAL GLAZE AND CARDSTOCK. [2] CUT BLACK AND COLORED CARDSTOCK TO SIZE IN ORDER TO CREATE THE LOOK OF A RECORD. ADHERE PIECES WELL WITH AMPLE ADHESIVE. [3] EMBELLISH AS DESIRED. APPLY AN EVEN COAT OF DIMENSIONAL GLAZE TO CREATE THE SHINY LOOK OF A RECORD.

50 YEARS TOO LATE

**ANGIE HEAD
FRIENDSWOOD, TEXAS**

It was off to the Sock Hop for Angie's son, featured on this page looking his coolest. To help her focal-point image stand out, Angie printed one of her photos in color and then mounted it at an angle, among the other black-and-white images. Her title was created with chipboard letters covered in patterned paper and altered with chalk, with rub-ons used for the lower portion. A variety of arrow stickers create a rewind effect, emphasizing the fun of the title. Angie adhered handwritten journaling strips to her pull-out file folder and added lots of funky rub-ons to complete the retro theme.

Supplies: Patterned paper (BasicGrey); arrow stickers, chipboard numbers (EK Success); chipboard letters (Zsiage); rub-on letters (BasicGrey, EK Success); rub-ons (Maisy Mo, Making Memories); ribbon (Ribbon Girls); blank CD; diamond glaze; chalk ink; pen; cardstock

A KIND SOUL

KATHY FESMIRE
ATHENS, TENNESSEE

Of all the awards Kathy's daughter could have won upon graduating from sixth grade, Kathy could not have been more proud when her daughter received the Citizenship Award, and created this sentimental layout to celebrate her daughter's good-natured personality. She used black-and-white accents to stand apart from the joyful, dancing patterns, and included a large flower embellishment to add feminine flair. Large, hand-cut parentheses draw attention to Kathy's heartfelt journaling, which is balanced by the single sharp photo of her daughter with award in hand.

Supplies: Patterned paper (My Mind's Eye); chipboard letters (Heidi Swapp); letter stickers (Doodlebug Designs, EK Success); rub-ons (Making Memories); flower (Creative Co-op); corner punch (EK Success); ribbon (Offray); stamping ink; button; cardstock

INTERVIEWS

Interviews are a great way to add personal perspective to your journaling. Pose these questions to your child to get them talking. Years to come, you'll treasure both the silly and serious answers from your star student.

★ What is your favorite thing about school?
★ What did you learn this year?

★ Did you like your classmates and teachers this year? Why or why not?
★ What do you feel was your greatest accomplishment this year?
★ What was the first day of school like? What about the last?
★ What was the funniest thing that happened at school this year?
★ What was the ultimate best moment at school this year?
★ What newsworthy events happened in the world this year? How did those events make you feel?

NY AQUARIUM

LISA DIXON
EAST BRUNSWICK, NEW JERSEY

Lisa loves to chaperone her son's middle school field trips, and designed this page around their trip to the aquarium and the sights the students were to learn about. She was able to incorporate a large amount of images onto the page by creating a small row of 1" x 1½" (3cm x 4cm) photos into a border strip. Beside each larger photo, Lisa made journaling placards by covering 1¾" x 3¼" (4cm x 8cm) chipboard rectangles with printed school worksheets related to the theme. She then set a smaller patterned paper rectangle on top, which she overlaid with journaling printed onto vellum.

Supplies: Patterned paper (BasicGrey, Crate Paper); vellum; wooden letters (Li'l Davis Designs); distress ink; chipboard; science trip worksheet; cardstock

AWARDS

JENNIFER GALLACHER
AMERICAN FORK, UTAH

Chipboard stars and black star patterned paper help establish a star-studded sophistication on Jennifer's layout, paying tribute to the many awards her son received on Honor Day at his school. The black background sets the formal feel for the page, while decorative scissors create an energetic border for visual excitement. Machine stitching around the blue cardstock mat adds senti-mental softness, while black photo turns secure the look in style.

Supplies: Patterned paper (Autumn Leaves, K & Company); letter template (Gone Scrappin'); chipboard stars (Li'l Davis Designs); star stamp (source unknown); stamping ink; photo turns (7 Gypsies); circle punch; decorative scissors; brads, cardstock; Antique Type font (ScrapVillage)

SCHOOL DANCE
DENISE TUCKER
VERSAILLES, INDIANA

Vibrant colors and festive trims play up the excitement of a middle school dance on Denise's exuberant creation. A prism effect paint sprayed onto her blue cardstock establishes a high-spirited background to set the tone for the page, while a transparency sprayed with chrome paint provides additional shimmer. She captured the thrill of dressing up with floral and sequin borders and posh velvet ribbons. Denise used notebook-style paper for her computer journaling, adhered it to patterned paper and added a ribbon, so that it can be slipped from the window pocket that she created.

Supplies: Patterned paper (Autumn Leaves, BasicGrey, Rusty Pickle); transparency; floral trim (Wrights); ribbon (Offray); letters (Colorbok); metallic paint, plastic paint, paper protector (Krylon); sequins (Jewelcraft); staples; cardstock

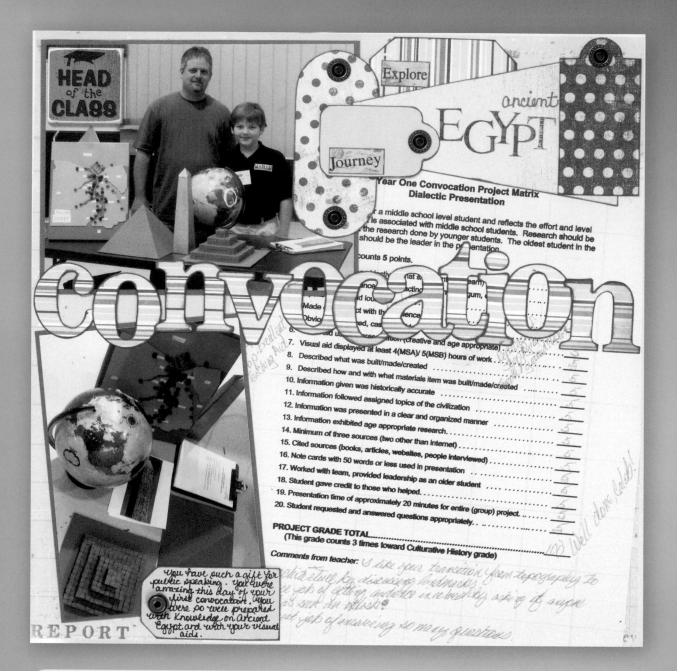

CONVOCATION

ANGIE HEAD
FRIENDSWOOD, TEXAS

To commemorate her son's first convocation, Angie printed a copy of Caleb's grading matrix directly onto a patterned paper that would mesh with the other papers and photos in her layout. While her title was made with letter masks as stencils and patterned paper, a subtitle was created in the upper right through a tag collage, rivets and letter stickers. Chalk ink was added to both title letters and tags for definition.

Supplies: Patterned paper (Autumn Leaves, BasicGrey, Crate Paper, Making Memories); rivets (Chatterbox); sticker labels (Bo-Bunny Press, K & Company); letter stickers (K & Company); letter masks (Heidi Swapp); chipboard (Bazzill); chalk ink; pen; cardstock

STAR QUIZZER

SHARON LAAKKONEN
SUPERIOR, WISCONSIN

Wanting to honor her son's best year ever in quiz competitions, Sharon created this simple expression of acclamation to treasure Billy's prestigious accomplishments and leadership abilities. Kraft paper cardstock lends a neutral background to the page, allowing the colossal look of the patterned paper star to serve as the shining force behind the photos. The stellar theme is repeated throughout the page with chipboard and acrylic stars twinkling around Sharon's star quizzer.

Supplies: Patterned paper (Chatterbox); chipboard shapes (Heidi Swapp); acrylic stars, mini brads, letter brads (Queen & Co.); pen; thread; cardstock

BRAINS & BEAUTY

KITTY FOSTER,
SNELLVILLE, GEORGIA

Awards for both grades and character were received by Hannah at her middle school award ceremony, and this layout expresses her parents' pride for the ways their daughter shines. To create the page, Kitty overlapped 2" x 6" (5cm x 15cm) photos of her daughter's awards and adhered them to the page, matted onto floral background paper. She folded a 5" x 12" (13cm x 30cm) strip of cardstock in half, printing her journaling on the inside right and adding a 5" x 6" image (13cm x 15cm) on the inside left. The top fold of the paper was covered with another 5" x 6" (13cm x 15cm) photo, accentuated with a chipboard circle, covered with gray paper and a printed ampersand.

Supplies: Patterned paper, border stickers, tab sticker, die-cut letters (My Mind's Eye); chalk ink; chipboard; cardstock

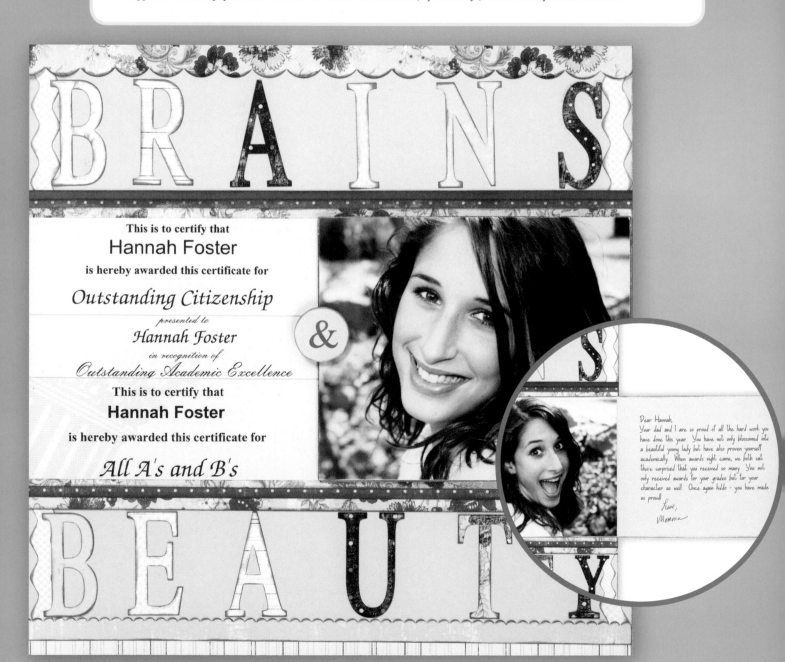

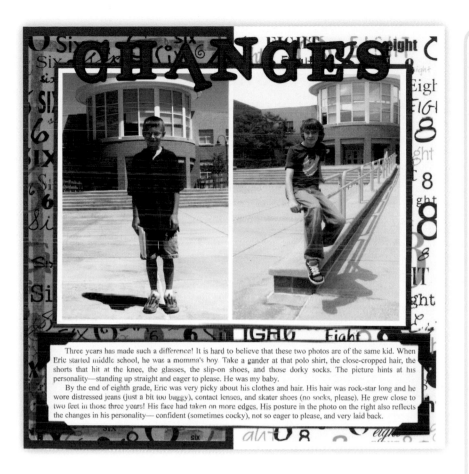

CHANGES

KELLI NOTO
CENTENNIAL, COLORADO

From awkward-stage sixth grader to confident rock star, side-by-side comparison photos mark the dramatic changes in Kelli's son, Eric, upon entering and leaving middle school. Kelli kept the page simple to allow the photos to share the wonders of change. She used black and white printed vellum on either side of the page to enhance the night-and-day appearances, as well as to share the differing grade numbers in the print. Kelli used die-cut letters and photo corners in red to unify the look, while keeping the red shirt in the left photo from overpowering the page.

Supplies: Patterned vellum (Flair Designs); die-cut letters and shapes (QuicKutz); cardstock

REPORT CARD HOLDER

LISA DIXON
EAST BRUNSWICK, NEW JERSEY

Gone are the days of receiving sturdy handwritten report cards housed in yellow manila envelopes. Lisa says her kids now come home waving thin sheets of computer-generated paper containing their grades. In her true creative spirit, she constructed a mini report card holder out of a pre-made stitched file folder. In addition to holding report cards, the folder also contains her daughter's class schedule, school papers and other tidbits. A mixture of patterned papers, ribbons, fibers, stickers, chipboard accents, envelopes, tags, labels and photographs turn the folder into a keepsake that is perfect for capturing a student's school year from beginning to end.

Supplies: File folder (Junkitz); patterned paper, chipboard letters and accents (We R Memory Keepers); ribbons, trims (Imagination Project, May Arts, Ribbon Smyth, Rusty Pickle); solvent ink; distress ink; fabric accents (Offray), number stickers (Bo-Bunny Press); letter stickers (BasicGrey); letter stamps (PSX Design); bookplate (Making Memories); shapeable thread (Scrapworks); tag (Avery); pen; eyelets; school worksheets; AL Modern Type font (Two Peas in a Bucket)

ProM

She couldn't have looked more beautiful on her Senior Prom night. She spent an evening laughing and dancing with friends. She had more fun than she ever thought she'd have.

Four years of high school and achievement have culminated to this special night, followed closely by graduation. A night exceeding all expectations could not have been a better reward.

06

CHAPTER 4

GOING PLACES
[Grades 9 – 12]

As if allowing this walking, talking extension of your heart to enter preschool wasn't hard enough, hold on; now it's time for high school. And this wild ride of life speeds up. Feel blessed to be part of the process as your somewhat awkward, often insecure, Freshman unfolds into the shining and sure Senior you always knew was meant to be. Hold on to each moment as a celebration of life, as together with your teen you laugh, feel anxious, cry a little and rejoice a lot. The finishing years of high school are nearly as exciting to scrapbook as your child's first steps. As your child learns to walk as a young adult in high school, he or she will be prepared to begin to run the race of life. Capture those sporting events, prom nights and, of course, graduation to send your child off into the real world with wings. May the love you pour into each page give your child the ability to not merely fly...but to soar.

ARE YOU READY?

TARGET

shine

EASY AS
1.2.3
ONE, TWO, THREE

?

Since when does a girl need an excuse to go shopping? Rosa actually never does, but back to school definitely qualifies. And, where is her favorite place for everything she needs? Target! Not only does it have the very best, hippest inventory around, it's just plain fun to shop there! The colorful displays, the yummy popcorn, that cute little dog; I mean, what more could she want? Rosa had such a great time picking out notebooks, a new school bag, a super cute head scarf; just about all her back to school "essentials". I'm so excited for her to start her Senior year. I remember what a special time it was. So, I think she's ready now: items are checked off the list, a new outfit laid out, a fresh haircut. Watch out, Levine Senior High School! (August, 2006)

"ARE YOU READY?"

KIM KESTI
PHOENIX, ARIZONA

Bright colors and fresh papers are all a fun part of shopping for back-to-school supplies, and Kim used both in this layout filled with the anticipation of her daughter's senior year. Kim grouped all of her photos together in a block, keeping the many colors coordinated. Her title makes an exaggerated statement of joy along the top, with a patterned paper shooting star used for funky flair. Printed journaling nicely fills the white space along the right, while trendy teen accents continue the youthful energy of the design.

Supplies: Patterned paper (Provo Craft, SEI); cardstock stickers (Provo Craft); conchos, letter stickers, rub-on, word stickers (Scrapworks); vellum; pen; cardstock; Arial font (Microsoft)

SEPTEMBER STYLIN'

SHARON LAAKKONEN
SUPERIOR, WISCONSIN

Brittany loves back-to-school shopping more than Sharon's other girls do, and this retro-style page showcases this school year's favorite finds. Sharon drew her colors and patterns from the outfits in the photos, which she set at an angle for visual interest and framed in cardstock. Hand-stitching, coordinating buttons and cork flowers all accessorize the frame in style, with journaling strips and a file tab accent balancing out opposing corners.

Supplies. Patterned paper (BasicGrey, Imagination Project); buttons (Autumn Leaves); cork flowers (Prima); brads (Queen & Co.); chipboard letters, file tab (Imagination Project); embroidery floss; dye ink; cardstock; Bliss font (Two Peas in a Bucket)

SCHOOL DAY STYLE

Want to make your pages too cool for school? Give your school-day creations scholastic style with these fun ideas and supplies.

- ★ Ledger or notebook paper
- ★ Mathematical equations
- ★ Clothing labels
- ★ Images of books, pencils or apples
- ★ Rulers (ribbon, twill or border sticker)
- ★ Large type in primary colors

...uniFORM

Attending Savannah Christian means one sure thing--uniform! For Katie that means a crisp white button-collar shirt with pockets, a short red, plaid skirt, knee socks, and dress shoes. We had a discussion once about our feelings about uniforms, and we agree. YUCK! Still, everyone else has to suffer through just like Katie; and that must help to make it more bearable. The one positive thing about her uniform was the cherished and much anticipated end-of-school tradition of having your good friends sign your shirt with a permanent marker and ripping your skirt. Is there anything like having permission to be rebellious?

Good Luck Katie-Claire

UNIFORM

JENNIFER GALLACHER
AMERICAN FORK, UTAH

While Katie may not understand the purpose behind her high school's uniforms, this graphic-style layout emphasizes her good-natured perseverance and the anticipation of destroying the outfits at the end of the year. Jennifer pulled her color scheme from the hues found in the plaid uniform skirt, and kept a clean and crisp look to match the outfit with straight lines and minimal embellishment. A band of simple eyelets separate the photos and the journaling, while adding a hint of shine and dimension.

Supplies: Patterned paper (My Mind's Eye); chipboard letters (Heidi Swapp); punctuation accents (Doodlebug Designs, EK Success); eyelets (Making Memories); cardstock

LOCKER BULLETIN BOARD

JESSIE BALDWIN
LAS VEGAS, NEVADA

Sassy and saucy, flirty and fun—this locker bulletin board is perfect for the modern girl navigating her way through the halls of high school. A fusion of color pops from a background of ribbon, rickrack, flowers, brads, magnetic buttons and inspirational phrases. A little bit sugar, a little bit spice, all the elements come together to create a chic item she'll love to show off. A miniature calendar adds the ultimate finishing touch perfect for an energetic girl with a flair for teen adventure.

Supplies: Ribbon (May Arts, Maya Road, Offray); brads, swirl clips (Creative Impressions); flowers (Queen & Co.); woven tag (Me & My Big Ideas); word plates (Making Memories); "all about me" tag (Around the Block); buttons; magnets; cork board; magnetic board

NIKE

DENISE TUCKER
VERSAILLES, INDIANA

An annual trip to the outlet mall is a fun way for Denise's family to say good-bye to summer and hello to new Nike wear! This all-boy layout commemorates her family's favorite back-to-school event, with an athletic-gear company logo printed onto a transparency and then heat embossed with thick powder, setting the tone for the page. A number strip set beside her focal-point photo serves as a unique means to signify her son's age, using a round metal label holder to circle the number, and decoupage medium to fill in the recess. Denise created the unique vintage look on her printed file tab by first inking the tab using plastic wrap and a sponge applicator.

Supplies: Patterned paper (Daisy D's); transparency; paper protector (Krylon); rickrack (Rusty Pickle); rivets (Chatterbox); round bookplate (7 Gypsies); charm (Around the Block); decoupage medium; embossing powder; distress ink; string; brand logo (Internet download)

CREATE CUSTOM PAPER CLIPS

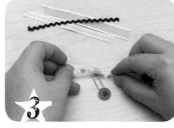

[1] ATTACH PAPER CLIP TO TAG. (NOTE: TAG COMES WITH ADHESIVE DOT ON BACK.) PUNCH WHITE CARDSTOCK CIRCLE AND PLACE OVER ADHESIVE DOT TO SECURE PAPER CLIP TO TAG. [2] PUNCH COLORED CIRCLE FROM SCRAPS OF PAPER. ADD RUB-ON LETTERS AND EPOXY STICKERS TO SOME; ADD EPOXY LETTERS TO OTHERS. [3] ADD RIBBON AS DESIRED. ATTACH TO PAGE.

DRESS CODE

KATHY FESMIRE
ATHENS, TENNESSEE

It was a rude awakening for Alexandra's closet upon entering high school. Her school's strict dress code may not have made Alexandra happy, but Kathy had great fun making this page. To contrast the solid colors and simple dress style of her daughter's school, Kathy used bold colors and opposing patterns in this layout. Rub-ons and letter stickers take a playful stab at the journaling strips, which express the particulars of the dress code. She made a whimsical title as a stand-alone element by employing varying colors and styles of chipboard letters accentuated with epoxy letters set in typewriter keys on paper clips.

Supplies: Patterned paper (My Mind's Eye); adhesive tags, stickers, doodle rub-ons (EK Success); epoxy stickers (Paper Studio); rub-on letters (Karen Foster Design); letter stickers (Doodlebug Designs); chipboard letters (BasicGrey, EK Success, Li'l Davis Designs); ribbons (American Crafts, Offray); dye ink; acrylic paint; foam adhesive spacers; decoupage medium; paper clips

DANA HILLS HIGH SCHOOL

SUZY PLANTAMURA
LAGUNA NIGUEL, CALIFORNIA

High school was a whole new world for Thane, who found he actually loved his new status and school, despite his expectations. Suzy created this page to commemorate her son's milestone moment, arriving at Freshmen orientation. She composed her unique background by enlarging three photos of Thane's school to 12" (30cm) wide and then cropping to 4" (10cm) high for a stacked panoramic effect. She softened the look of the background with a sheet of 12" x 12" (30cm x 30cm) vellum, and cut a pocket into the top of the bottom photo to place the school year's class schedule and her son's Freshman ID card. A word-themed paper clip fastens the two together with simplistic style.

Supplies: Vellum; rub-ons (7 Gypsies, Die Cuts With A View, Li'l Davis Designs); fabric tags (Scrapworks); paper clip (Adorn It); chipboard letter (Target); fine point marker; solvent ink

6:30a – When it's not Water Polo Season, this is when I wake up. I'm feeling groggy, but mom always makes a great breakfast.

7:21a - The exact time to leave for catching the bus; we've got it down to a science. Mom has to drive me to the bus stop since it's across the street from BevMo.

8:00a - School starts. First Period/Geometry. To be honest, it's hard to go wrong in my math class. My teacher is nice, the material is easy for me, and I've got some buddies in the class. It's a good brain warm-up to start my day.

8:55a - Second Period/Biology. My teacher is awesome! Even though much of the class involves busywork (studying vocabulary, listening to lectures, etc.) all the work we do in the lab (dissections, microscope work) is worth it.

9:48a - 9:55a - Break: TOO SHORT! Only 7 minutes! I get some food from a vending machine, talk to friends, and take the usual trip to my locker to get the material for my next few classes.

10:00a - Third Period/Video Production: We watch movies and make our own, incorporating some of the camera techniques we notice. Cool teacher; old and liberal.

10:55a - Fourth Period/History: My water polo coach is the teacher. All of the "polo boys" call him "Mastah James" everyone else in my class has to call him Mr. Lathrop. I really like history class and we do a lot of fun activities (mostly watching historical or history-based movies or doing simulations that mirror the processes of different economical systems).

11:45a - 12:20p - LUNCH. Off to the field to play Ultimate Frisbee with my H²O Polo buddies. I learned to bring shoes; the astroturf gets really hot and gives you giant blisters.

12:25p - Fifth Period/English: I love my English teacher. She is very funny, and besides the fact that she teaches phenomenally and has helped me improve my writing, she is very nice and builds the self-esteem of everyone in her class.

1:20p - Sixth Period/P.E: I think PE is a joke and we shouldn't have to do it, but it can be fun.

2:15p - Seventh Period/Spanish: I love the Spanish language and culture, and I try my hardest to pay attention during this end-of-the-day class.

3:05p - School Ends.

more →

BRIAN'S DAY
life as a freshman

2005 - 2006

BR

BRIAN'S DAY (LIFE AS A FRESHMAN)

KATHLEEN SUMMERS
ROSEVILLE, CALIFORNIA

A day in the life of Kathleen's freshman nephew unfolds on this less-is-more layout. Kathleen kept the right side of the page clean and uncomplicated, allowing the school-themed images on photo real stickers and photos from her nephew's world to speak boldly against the stark white background. She used her computer to create her title, as well as the "more" circle, which used reverse printing technique. The hour-by-hour journaling on the right opens like a card, with magnetic "snaps" used to hold it closed.

Supplies: Border sticker (Memories Complete); photo stickers (Me & My Big Ideas); number stamps (Hero Arts); stamping ink; magnetic snaps (BasicGrey); cardstock

DECISIONS, DECISIONS

KIM MORENO
TUCSON, ARIZONA

Striped-pattern papers in bold and brilliant colors recreate the look of the many clothes to be found in Brandy's wardrobe! Kim added a polka-dot pattern circle beneath her photo arrangement, adding a contradicting element in coordinating colors to create an overwhelming feeling of confusion, much like this teenager's decisions about outfits. Kim painted a wire flower accent to mesh with the page and set it in place with a yellow brad. A single chipboard letter in her lower title block gives dimension and playfulness. Kim's journaling, printed on a transparency and layered over patterned paper, gently teases her sister about the "rough decisions" to be made in the life of a teenage girl.

Supplies: Patterned paper, letter stickers, chipboard letter (Scenic Route Paper Co.); arrow turns (7 Gypsies); chipboard frames (Pressed Petals); letter stamps (EK Success, PSX Design); metal flowers (Maya Road); brads; stamping ink; pen; cardstock

AFTER SCHOOL RITUAL

SUZY PLANTAMURA
LAGUNA NIGUEL, CALIFORNIA

Suzy's all-American boy is the star of this after-school traditions page, which showcases Thane's daily rituals. Number word stickers take the viewer step-by-step through each of Thane's post-school activities, with white pen used to journal the details. Suzy used die-cut stars from varying patterned papers to lend a visual energy, which she coordinated in the stellar ribbon borders as well. The use of visual triangles creates a well-balanced composition, through the photo arrangement and placement of the stars.

Supplies: Patterned paper (BasicGrey, Scenic Route Paper Co.); chipboard letters (Heidi Swapp); die-cut stars (Provo Craft); stickers (EK Success); ribbon (source unknown); dye ink; pen

Within the layout:

aFTeR schOOL RitUal

"Thane is such a creature of habit. Every day after school he has a "ritual".

my favorite things

ONE

J. Mc
2006

First, it's snack time - usually the same thing. He eats Wheat Thins and cream cheese and a whipped Yoplait yogurt. It must be key lime pie or lemon meringue.

TWO

The T.V. must be on - usually a hockey game. Then he goes up to his room and does his homework. Last, he goes outside to play hockey with friends.

THREE

ART TIME

SHARON LAAKKONEN
SUPERIOR, WISCONSIN

When Brittany's parents asked her to customize her art class to fit her interests, she immediately fell in love with a new-found passion for scrapbooking. Sharon incorporated photos that Brittany had applied digital filters to on this layout, as well as the decorative floral embellishments her daughter made. Cork flower accents balance the upper portion of the page in coordinating style, while hand-stitches of embroidery floss lend textural details and doodling.

Supplies: Patterned paper (American Crafts, Chatterbox, Provo Craft); cork flowers (Prima); letter stickers, label (Chatterbox); rub-ons (BasicGrey); acrylic flowers, brads (Queen & Co.); pen; fine point marker; embroidery floss; dye ink; thread; image editing software (Adobe); cardstock

CAUGHT SPEEDING

DENISE TUCKER
VERSAILLES, INDIANA

Denise pauses the rotating wheels of time on this car-themed creation. Denise featured a photo of her son with his newly acquired driver's license, used a car-patterned paper to set the tone, and added racing striped ribbon borders and actual toy car tires to further the effect. Wistfully, Denise added her dates on yellow patterned paper set inside round metal label tabs, filled with decoupage to create a yellow traffic light accent. To further the "speeding through life" theme, Denise scanned a Traffic Violation Notification to use as the background for her pull-out journaling.

It seems like just a few years ago that you were thrilled by the car Santa left for you under the tree. Today, you have finished your driver's education classes, put in your time driving with a permit, and are now able to drive freely with your friends. My prayer for you is that your guardian angels will continue to be vigilant, and that the bumps ahead on life's road will be smooth. Also, I ask that, for your Mom's sake, you tap on those brakes and slow down your speeding habits just a little.

Supplies: Patterned paper, chipboard letter (Rusty Pickle); embossing powder; metallic stickers (Mrs. Grossman's); ribbon (Scrap Therapy); fabric letters (Adorn It); labels (Dymo); metal index tabs (7 Gypsies); acrylic paint; decoupage medium; paper protector (Krylon); toy tires; speeding ticket (Internet download); cardstock

in one day
LIFE
IS WHAT YOU MAKE IT
Jeff took on the job of landscaping a needy family's house because it would look good on his college resume... but by the time the project was over, he realized he took part in changing a family's life. What a difference a day makes!
volunteer
Super star

IN ONE DAY

JESSIE BALDWIN
LAS VEGAS, NEVADA

The act of landscaping the house of a family in need began as a means for Jeff to improve his college resume, but ended as a way to his heart by seeing the way a volunteer can make a difference. Jessie designed this celebration of character-building using masculine tones of greens, blues and browns. She established a unique border in the middle of her photos by layering die-cut tags. Handwritten journaling on notebook paper gives contrast to the busy designs and adds a student-themed style.

Supplies: Patterned paper, die-cuts (Fancy Pants Designs); letter stickers (American Crafts); marker; notebook paper

PHOTOS

KIM KESTI
PHOENIX, ARIZONA

In honor of Photography, her daughter's favorite subject, Kim created this layout around Meghan's own photo samples. Kim included several of her daughter's black-and-white images from class to support the theme, and added one of her contact sheets as well. In the upper page portion, Kim used a metal label holder to frame several shots, which she fastened with colorful brads to mesh with the patterned paper. The focal photo was kept in color to stand out on the page, and the shape of the camera lens in the image is repeated in the patterned paper border and the matching handmade accents on the left.

Supplies: Patterned paper (Cherry Arte); bookplate (Li'l Davis Designs); long brads (Junkitz); stickers (Memories Complete); circle punch; stamping ink; cardstock; Times New Roman font

Photos ended up being Meghan's favorite class her Senior year. She really "got into" the whole idea; taking photos, developing her own film, and even printing in the darkroom. Maybe I'm biased, but I think she took some really great photos! Great job, girl! (May, 2006)

PHOTO CHECKLIST

★ 4-year high school overview
★ Senior portraits
★ Freshman to Senior transformations
★ School dress codes
★ School mascots
★ Afterschool rituals
★ Driver's license milestone
★ First car
★ Prom
★ Sports season overviews
★ Grown-up moments
★ Graduation ceremonies
★ Graduation parties and celebrations

CHEROKEES

KATHY FESMIRE
ATHENS, TENNESSEE

In awe of the gorgeous piece of artwork on her children's high school sign, Kathy devoted an entire layout to this proud mascot. She kept the layout simple, using only a photo of the mascot and the high school's sign. Ribbons chosen in the school's colors of black and gold give texture and visual interest to the page, while feathers and beaded trim play up the theme. Her pull-out, handwritten journaling is tucked behind the photo of the school sign.

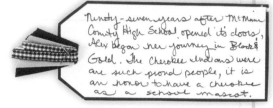

Ninety-seven years after McMinn County High School opened it's doors, Alex began her journey in Black & Gold. The Cherokee Indians were are such proud people, it is an honor to have a cherokee as a school mascot.

Supplies: Cardstock; rub-ons (Me & My Big Ideas); letter stickers (EK Success); letter stamps (Magnetic Poetry); ribbons (Offray); acrylic paint; staples; pen

MY PLANNER

HEATHER PRECKEL
SWANNANOA, NORTH CAROLINA

The active life of a teen is rarely tempered with a moment of down time. Classes, activities and friends take center stage in an adolescent's world, often necessitating the need for schedules and time tables. To remedy the chaos, Heather created a bright and bold Day Planner for the dynamic student on-the-go. She covered the front of the Planner with coordinating patterned papers and polka-dot ribbon. The repetition of geometric shapes adds movement while the bright colors add vibrancy and energy. A metal bookplate secured with mini brads completes the look.

Supplies: Notebook (Target); patterned paper (Provo Craft); bookplate (Daisy D's); ribbon (May Arts); brads; decorative tape (7 Gypsies); pen

YOU CALL IT HOME, WE CALL IT SCHOOL

**BARB HOGAN
CINCINNATI, OHIO**

To capture the non-traditional flavor of the homeschooling lifestyle, Barb cooked up this "free-style" tribute to her friend's teenagers in their learning groove. Barb cut and inked her photos and chose energetic patterned paper in vibrant hues, which she tore and inked for funky festivity. A buckle adorned with ribbons on the left adds a textural statement of creativity and cool. Barb printed her journaling on a library card to play up the educational element, while handwriting and doodles on both background and photos create youthful excitement and fun.

Supplies: Patterned paper (7 Gypsies, BasicGrey, Deja Views, Design Originals, SEI, We R Memory Keepers); letter stickers (Arctic Frog); cardstock stickers (Pebbles); brads (Making Memories); buckle (Junkitz); ribbon (May Arts, Michaels, Offray); library card (Daisy D's); pigment ink; pen; fine point marker; cardstock

PLAYING WATER POLO MEANS...

KATHLEEN SUMMERS
ROSEVILLE, CALIFORNIA

The fun of water polo, in her nephew's terms, makes a splash on Kathleen's dedication page to Brian's high school passion. Handcut arrows from cool, pool-inspired papers take the viewer on a journey through the perks and quirks of this adored aquatic sport in Brian's particular school. A curvy, angled border set along the left pulls the layout together with the arrows and furthers the water-based theme, while dots drawn around the elements give poolside pizzazz and a winsome touch.

Supplies: Patterned paper (Karen Foster Design); letter stickers (Arctic Frog); pen; cardstock

WITH HONORS

KELLI NOTO
CENTENNIAL, COLORADO

Though she had no qualms about her son graduating from high school, Kelli created this formal celebration layout to applaud his receipt of top honors. Pulling out the blue and black from the cap and gown, Kelli combined coordinating cardstock, patterned paper and die-cut letters to compose this uncomplicated design. Cardstock strips set along the borders lend a graphic edge and establish a subtle frame against the stark black background. Patterned paper set at an angle gives a well-balanced excitement to the design.

Supplies: Patterned paper (Adorn It); die-cut letters and numbers (QuicKutz); self-adhesive clear computer paper (ChartPak); cardstock

TICKET TO CHANGE

KIM KESTI
PHOENIX, ARIZONA

Wanting to highlight her daughter's graduation with a unique title, Kim used the quote from Meghan's graduation announcement for her journaling, and then incorporated chipboard letters to stand out as her title. Silhouette stars dance in jubilation around the photo of the graduate and enhance the celebratory theme of the layout. Kim kept the background fairly simple, layering just a few patterned papers in non-obtrusive colors. An actual name card from her daughter's graduation invitations furthers the magic of this milestone moment.

Supplies: Patterned paper (Cherry Arte, Imagination Project); chipboard letters (Imagination Project); stars (Heidi Swapp); staples; acrylic paint; cardstock; Arial font (Microsoft)

FIRST CAR

SHARON LAAKKONEN
SUPERIOR, WISCONSIN

Picking out her first car was a family event for Bethany, who wanted and chose something fun yet practical. Sharon documented the occasion here on this blissful page, showcasing Bethany's new ride, as well as the joy of family involvement in such a monumental decision. Sharon chose patterned papers with hints of the maroon-car color, and added a coordinating chipboard heart. Hand-doodling on the heart and chipboard letters give the page a festive flair, and mimic the machine stitching along the borders.

Supplies: Patterned paper (American Crafts, Imagination Project); chipboard letters, heart, letter stickers (Imagination Project); brads (Queen & Co.); dye ink; thread; pen; cardstock

PEACE OUT

BARB HOGAN
CINCINNATI, OHIO

Shying away from a traditional, formal page, Barb let her creativity run wild to capture the exhilaration of high school graduation. She created this edgy look and feel by combining strips of coordinating, kinesthetic patterns with matching circles and rings to bounce about the design. License plate letters, set at varying angles, play with ink-smudged letter stickers to hype up the title. The celebratory feel is further enhanced through explosive doodles drawn with white pen, handwritten journaling on black cardstock strips and shapes randomly placed in festive fun.

Supplies: Patterned paper (Rusty Pickle, We R Memory Keepers); letter stickers (Imagination Project, Sticker Studio); circle punch; solvent ink; pen; cardstock

MEMORABILIA

Looking for some fun items to include on a layout about your teen? With so many events and milestones during the high school years, you're sure to collect a treasure trove of items you can incorporate into your pages. Here are some cool ideas:

★ Certificates, ribbons, awards or varsity letter
★ Notes from classmates and teachers
★ Report card or class schedule
★ Special test scores
★ School bumper stickers or pennants
★ Programs or fliers from special events
★ Receipts

★ Photocopies of school images, logos, pledges, etc.
★ High school diploma
★ Favorite clothing labels
★ Copies of textbook covers
★ Birthday or graduation cards
★ Newspaper clippings

PROM

AMBER BALEY
WAUPUN, WISCONSIN

No greater reward could have come for Whitney, after four years of hard work and high school achievement, than a prom night that far exceeded her wildest dreams. Amber captured the beauty of the event in this dazzling display of formality and fun. She created her own background pattern by cutting black cardstock into diamonds and adhering them to white cardstock. She counterbalanced the straight edges of the pattern with a free-flowing flower cut from patterned paper and enhanced with black ink and paint. Rub-on flourishes, a free-spirited bird and swirly, metal photo corners continue the dreamy illusion, while a torn paper wave dances along the bottom, balancing the opposing angle in the photo.

Supplies: Patterned paper (7 Gypsies, My Mind's Eye); transparency; chipboard letters (Heidi Swapp); rub-ons (BasicGrey); photo corners (source unknown); acrylic paint; solvent ink; dimensional glaze; thread; cardstock; Georgia font (Dafont)

She couldn't have looked more **beautiful** on her Senior Prom night. She spent an evening **laughing** and **dancing** with friends. She had more **fun** than she ever thought she'd have.

Four years of high school and **achievement** have culminated to this **special** night, followed closely by graduation. A night exceeding all **expectations** could not have been a better **reward**.

BEAUTIFUL

**KATHY FESMIRE
ATHENS, TENNESSEE**

Elegant beauty graces Kathy's page, dedicated to the thrill of a senior prom. Kathy chose white, pearly buttons, ribbons and flower details to create a simple display of sweet sophistication, without distracting from the photo taken before the event. A hidden journaling tag resides behind the photo, easily accessible by a delicate ribbon. The black photo corners and flowing script printed on the white paper add contrast to the design.

Prom night is always so special. After having their pictures taken in these gorgeous gardens, Jared and Shay headed to Knoxville for their prom night. Pictures and dancing were followed by dinner at the Copper Cellar to help create a prom night they will never forget.

Supplies: Cardstock; flowers (Creative Co-op); photo corners; ribbon (Offray); buttons (source unknown)

DECORATED FRAME

**AMBER BALEY
WAUPUN, WISCONSIN**

Amber created this charming frame to display the beautiful senior portrait of her young friend. She started by covering the frame's edges with floral, striped and checked patterned papers. She created the fun flower in the upper left corner using circle die-cuts and a flower punch. Amber sanded the edges and slightly bent the petals to give the flower dimension. A chipboard monogram and numbers shine with an application of dimensional glaze while ribbon and mini tags add the final touch.

Supplies: Patterned paper, stickers (My Mind's Eye); button (Junkitz); rub-ons, ribbon (Chatterbox); brad (Queen & Co.); chipboard numbers (Heidi Swapp); chipboard letter (Grafix); die-cut tag (Sizzix); die-cut flowers (Provo Craft); flower punch; sandpaper, twine

Katie DAD

DANCE

save me a

It's hard for
every dad to
see their little
girl grow up,
even if it
is into a
beautiful young
woman. How
lucky you are
to have a Dad
that loves you
so very much!
Katie and her
Father share a
dance at Prom.

SAVE ME A DANCE

JENNIFER GALLACHER
AMERICAN FORK, UTAH

A unique twist on the traditional prom-theme page, Jennifer designed this fun yet formal layout around the high school's tradition of allowing parents to come to the first half of prom to dance with their children. Jewel tone colors and luxurious patterns capture the rich emotion found in both the event and parental pride. Shimmering jewels dance among paper flowers and translucent twinkling stars to create a glamorous corsage collage in the upper right, while a handful of flowers balance the look in the lower left.

Supplies: Patterned paper (Deja Views, Karen Foster Design); mini labels, border, file tabs, die-cut letters (Deja Views); letter stamps (Karen Foster Design, PSX Design); stamping ink; stars (Heidi Swapp); flowers (Making Memories, Prima); brads; rhinestones; rhinestone brads (Karen Foster Design); cardstock; Antique Type font (ScrapVillage)

VARSITY 2005-06

DENISE TUCKER
VERSAILLES, INDIANA

Denise is on the ball in commemorating her son's varsity season, here on this awesome, aesthetic design. The layout is given a masculine, sporty look through the use of basketball-textured paper, staples, screw-themed brads and inked fabric strips. Denise created her own basketball, stained-glass transparency. Though it took nearly an entire day for the design to dry completely, the results definitely scored!

Supplies: Patterned paper, chipboard album cover (Rusty Pickle); textured basketball paper (Freckle Press); transparency; page protector spray (Krylon); ink-jet canvas (Fredrix); letter stamps (Making Memories); brads (Karen Foster Design); faux stone paint; stained glass paint; silver leafing pen; decoupage medium; solvent ink; distress ink; staples

CREATE THE LOOK OF STAINED GLASS

[1] SPRAY TRANSPARENCY SHEET WITH STAINED GLASS PAINT. SET ASIDE AND ALLOW TO DRY. [2] TRIM CIRCLE FROM CARDSTOCK WITH CRAFT KNIFE. [3] TRIM TRANSPARENCY AND ADHERE TO BACK OF CARDSTOCK. [4] APPLY DECOUPAGE MEDIUM TO ADD DIMENSION AND SHINE. USE A POINTED EMBOSSING TOOL TO DRAG THE MEDIUM INTO TIGHT CORNERS FOR CLEAN EDGES.

HIGH SCHOOL FAVORITES

KIM KESTI
PHOENIX, ARIZONA

Four years of high school converge creatively here on Kim's layout, which commemorates her daughter's very successful high school career of coursework in a unique keepsake overview. Kim placed her daughter's Four Year Plan in a page protector on the layout, and used colorful conchos to highlight Meghan's favorite classes. Small photo images downloaded from the Internet were set along the right-hand edge to illustrate the subject matter of several classes.

Supplies: Patterned paper, brads (Making Memories); flash card (7 Gypsies); conchos, rub-ons (Scrapworks); photos, acrylic sticker (source unknown); page protector; cardstock

*HIGH SCHOOL favorites

KESTI, MEGHAN E

GLENDALE UNION HIGH SCHOOL DISTRICT
APOLLO HIGH SCHOOL
8045 N 47TH AV
GLENDALE, ARIZONA 85302
623-435-6300 FAX 623-435-6369

Print Date: 08/29/05
CTDS NUMBER: 070505206
Counselor: TREIBER Entry Date: 081902 DATE OF GRAD: - -
GPA 3.9722, HPA 5.6389, CPA 3.9643; Class Rank: Top 2% of 450; Diploma: ENDORSE...

YR-Q	Course Title	G	Crd	R	RT	YR-Q	Course Title	G	Crd	R	RT
03-2	054306 KEYBOARD 1	1	.5	O		103-4	054406 KEYBOARD 2	1	.5	O	
03-2	062706 SPANISH 1	1	.5	1		103-4	062806 SPANISH 2	1	.5	1	
03-2	090502 ACL ENG 1	1	.5	3		103-4	090602 ACL ENG 2	1	.5	3	
03-2	106302 ACL MATH 3	1	.5	4		103-4	106402 ACL MATH 4	1	.5	4	
03-2	118730 ACL MATH 1-2	P	1.	4		103-4	130602 PHYS ED 2G	1	.5	6	
03-2	130502 PHYS ED 1G	1	.5	6		103-4	141001 ACL BIO 2	1	.5	7	
03-2	140901 ACL BIO 1	1	.5	7			PRESENT 176				

YR-Q	Course Title	G	Crd	R	RT	YR-Q	Course Title	G	Crd	R	RT
04-2	063302 SPANISH 3	1	.5	1		104-4	063402 SPANISH 4	1	.5	1	
04-2	091103 ACL ENG 3	1	.5	3		104-4	091203 ACL ENG 4	1	.5	3	
04-2	113501 ACCL MATH	1	.5	4		104-4	113601 ACCL MATH	1	.5	4	
04-2	123501 PIANO	1	.5	5		104-4	123601 PIANO	1	.5	5	
04-2	141502 ACL CHEM 1	1	.5	7		104-4	141602 ACL CHEM 2	1	.5	7	
04-2	154114 W HIS/AZ G1	1	.5	8		104-4	154214 W HIS/AZ G2	1	.5	8	
							PRESENT 178				

YR-Q	Course Title	G	Crd	R	RT	YR-Q	Course Title	G	Crd	R	RT
05-2	043501 PHOTO 1	1	.5	5		105-4	043601 PHOTO 2	1	.5	5	
05-2	091702 ACL ENG 5	1	.5	3		105-4	091802 ACL ENG 6	1	.5	3	
05-2	110302 ACL PRE CAL	1	.5	4		105-4	110402 ACL PRE CAL	1	.5	4	
05-2	132502 SYS CONDIT	1	.5	6		105-4	132602 SYS CONDIT G	1	.5	6	
05-2	140302 AP BIO 1	1	.5	7		105-4	140402 AP BIO 2	2	.5	7	
05-2	152901 US/AZ HIS 1	1	.5	8		105-4	153001 US/AZ HIS 2	1	.5	8	
							PRESENT 177				

YR-Q	Course Title	G	Crd	R	RT	YR-Q	Course Title	G	Crd	R	RT
06-2	043701 PHOTO 3			5		106-4	043801 PHOTO 4			5	
06-2	092501 AP ENGLISH			3		106-4	092601 AP ENGLISH			3	
06-2	154501 AP US/AZ GOV			8		106-4	154601 AP US/AZ G			8	
06-2	164501 PUBLICATION			O		106-4	164601 PUBLICATION			O	

We're so proud of Meghan as she completes her High School career. It was interesting to review her Four Year Plan and see which classes she enjoyed and which she endured. She took on quite a heavy workload with Advanced Placement English, History and Biology, Accelerated Math and Chemistry plus Spanish, Photos, Physical Conditioning and Piano. I suppose it's no surprise that her Piano and P.E. classes were two of her favorites. But, overall, she really enjoyed High School and is looking forward to entering the Arizona State University College of Nursing on a full ride scholarship. Like I said, we are awfully proud of her! Congratulations, Meghan! (May 2006)

DEF:

Total credits earned: 19   **Official if signed and stamped** 1 OF 1

Bethany has looked forward to this year for so long. 2006 is a great year to graduate from high school! There are so many fun things to do as a senior-like grad pics!

Bethany

These are some of Bethany's favorite poses from those pics.

06

BETHANY, 2006

SHARON LAAKKONEN
SUPERIOR, WISCONSIN

Wanting to display her daughter's graduation photos in a unique and festive manner, Sharon used a photo collage program to arrange the images and add the shadow boxes. Complementary orange and blue, drawn from the photos, lend a vibrant beauty to the page, while carefree flowers and free-spirited patterns set an exuberant energy around the layout. Beads added to the hand-stitched date give texture and shine, while coordinating beads ornamenting flowers on the left balance out the design with finesse.

Supplies: Patterned paper (American Crafts, Chatterbox, Imagination Project); chipboard photo corners (Imagination Project); flowers (Prima); beads, embroidery floss (Michaels); photo collage software (LumaPix); pen; cardstock

REPORT CARD HOLDER

KATHY FESMIRE
ATHENS, TENNESSEE

Senior year is the pinnacle of high school. With so many memories and accomplishments to record, Kathy wanted to find the best format for documenting the qualities and talents of her special girl. This pre-made mini book turned out to be the perfect choice. Using a tender color palette of green, aqua, pink and beige, she simply added rub-ons, ribbon and a few extra delicate accents to give the album continuity. Handwritten journaling adds a personal touch and the repetition of the black elements throughout the book ties the black-and-white photos in with the softer tones of the album.

Supplies: Mini Book Kit (K & Company); rub-ons (Dee's Designs, Me & My Big Ideas); ribbons (Offray); acrylic letter stickers (source unknown); pen

TRENT'S GROWTH

DENISE TUCKER
VERSAILLES, INDIANA

Denise's colossal baby, now 16 years old, continues to top the charts and tower above his classmates at 6'6", 200 lbs! She made this layout as a reminder to always continue to grow within, comparing then and now images of Trent side-by-side. Denise made the unique name element by spraying blue glass letters with a stone-effect paint, layering with crackle paint and then a final red stained glass paint. The vibrant journaling block was printed on an envelope, which she then enhanced with patterned paper on the inside flap.

Supplies: Patterned paper (K & Company, Rusty Pickle); vellum; paper protector (Krylon); printable canvas (Fredrix); envelope; glass letters (Heidi Grace); letter stickers (Pebbles); label (Dymo); letter stamps (Making Memories); clear rubber accent (Shoe Talkers); ribbon (Offray); brads; texturizing paint; crackle paint; stained glass paint; stamping ink; distress ink; foam squares; key rings; cardstock; Courier New font (Microsoft)

GOING PLACES

SUZY PLANTAMURA
LAGUNA NIGUEL, CALIFORNIA

The end of high school is the beginning of new life for Jordan, who is celebrated here on this inspiring layout. To tone down the look of the distracting background elements in the focal-point image, Suzy used photo-editing software to transform the background to black-and-white. The large photo background was enlarged and cropped to create a panoramic image, which she softened by decreasing contrast and increasing brightness in her software. An arrow added to the edge of the accent photo helps to easily locate Jordan among the sea of caps and gowns.

Supplies: Patterned paper (Autumn Leaves); transparency; chipboard letters and accents (Heidi Swapp); ribbon (source unknown); acrylic paint; solvent ink; image editing software (Adobe)

Jordan graduated from Upland High School today. This is the beginning of her new life and she is definitely going places. After four years of good grades and being in Color Guard, she is ready to move on and start her life. This is such an exciting time, with so many different paths to take. What will she study? What will her career be? When will she get married and start a family? So many new things waiting to be discovered ... a wide road ahead of her. She is such a smart and beautiful girl; I know she will find her way and do something great with her life. Graduation is just the beginning ... her life is about to be discovered. 06/04

★ STAR STUDENTS ★
[Contributing Artists]

★ JESSIE BALDWIN ★ My favorite school memory is from kindergarten. The class went on a field trip to the county library and we all got our very own library cards! My teacher wrote my name on the back of my card and I was so excited to have it. I put it right in my pocket. Later that morning we went to the park to play and have snacks, and when we got back to the classroom my card was no longer in my pocket. I was devastated! When I got home from school, I cried on my mom's lap telling her how I had lost my brand new card. Then, all of a sudden, she pulled my very card out of her pocket! She was a teacher at the time, and her class happened to go to the same park that day. One of her students found the card and brought it to my mom! I still carry that same library card. There's just something special about it.

★ AMBER BALEY ★ I always loved Christmas at the small private high school I attended in Waupun, Wisconsin. The students would decorate their lockers with wrapping paper and bows to celebrate the Holidays. It was almost as if each locker was a present waiting to be opened. I couldn't help but feel the Spirit of Christmas when I peered at the rows of decorated lockers that lined the hallway.

★ LISA DIXON ★ In second grade I loved Reading, so I was excited to start our classroom reading groups. I can still picture the colorful bulletin board decorated with a large tree. Sitting in the branches were nests with pretty die cut birds, a different kind of bird for each group. There were bluebirds, robins, sparrows and wrens. I sat at my desk and wished with all my heart that my name was on a pretty bluebird. And it was!

★ KATHY FESMIRE ★ Growing up, both of my parents were teachers so I always had a great respect for the work that teachers do. My absolute favorite teacher was Mrs. Ethelene Davis, my sixth grade teacher. All good Southerners have unique and different sayings and Mrs. Davis was no exception. I will never forget her laughter as she would chime out "Good night, Nurse!!" and "Good gracious, Grandma!!" in the classroom. She made us laugh and helped us learn. I will never forget her.

★ KITTY FOSTER ★ Fifth grade was a year of horrible hair and bad fashion experiments. I was fashion road kill! Due to my discovery of plaid jumpers, vests and the curling iron, I lacked social activities, so I goofed off. However, it was nothing that my teacher, Mrs. Charba, couldn't handle. School to me was a social event; all that academic stuff just got in the way! Somehow, Mrs. Charba was able to work with me just the same.

★ JENNIFER GALLACHER ★

I recently came across a couple of old photos of me dancing with a young man at our elementary school Dance Festival. The look of utter disgust on my face tells the story of my absolute horror during this activity. He really was a nice young man, but the thought of touching a boy at that age, let alone holding his hand, made me sick! I still feel terrible that I made him feel badly, and if my little-girl mind had realized how much fun dancing with boys would become, I probably would have been a little less disgusted.

★ ANGIE HEAD ★

My fondest memories of school revolve around the last half of my senior year in high school. I started dating this really awesome guy around Christmastime that year. We went to all of the formal dances and graduated together. We fell in love and are happily married today!

★ BARB HOGAN ★

Fourth grade was the first year that I actually had any challenges to face in school. For the first time ever, I had a teacher that didn't like me. She was mean and ill tempered and I really didn't like her much either. It was the year that I had to learn some hard lessons about how to be a better student and how to be a good friend. Sadly, these lessons came with a bit of heartache and pain, but in the end, they helped mold me into a better person.

★ VANESSA HUDSON ★

My favorite subject in school was recess. Our playground was at the bottom of a giant hill. Our favorite thing to do was start at the top of the hill and roll all the way to the bottom, until we were so dizzy we couldn't stand up. Years passed, and one night after a senior basketball game, my best friend and I revisited the hill for one more roll, just like we were little kids again.

★ CAROLINE HUOT ★

My best school memories go back to the first day of school every year. Since my two cousins and I were in the same grade and same school, it was always a thrill to find out which cousin was in my class that particular year. Kindergarten was the only grade that we were all in the same class, and sixth grade was the only year that we were all separated.

★ KIM KESTI ★

Fourth grade was my absolute *funnest* year in school. It was the first year that I had a male teacher and he always had the best ideas. He even had a tower in the corner of our classroom, complete with a platform for reading. Since I was such a teacher's pet, I was able to earn plenty of "free reading time" up in the tower. It was also the year that I perfected cursive handwriting and covered every available surface with my flowing script. Ah, to be nine years old again would be lovely.

★ SHARON LAAKKONEN ★

My senior year was filled with excitement and anticipation. The graduation ceremony was the perfect ending for such a fun year. My mind raced over the past years as I half-listened to the speeches. I had so many questions. Was this really it for me? Was I really a graduate? What was ahead for me? As they announced my name and handed me my very own diploma, happiness radiated through me. I really had made it! Walking down the aisle at the end of the ceremony with my "now-hubby-Bill" was the icing on the cake!

★ BRENDA McANDREWS ★

Miss Ford was my first grade teacher. I loved being in her class. She was the nicest first grade teacher. I felt so at home around her I would sometimes slip and call her "Mom." I also enjoyed riding the bus with the big kids, including my two older sisters.

★ KIM MORENO ★

My favorite school memories revolve around playing sports. I played varsity volleyball, basketball, and ran track all through high school. Sports were an outlet for me. An outlet that helped me want to keep my grades up, kept me out of trouble (mostly), and where I made some of my best friends. I enjoyed volleyball the most. I played with the high school team and also club ball with the city and traveled throughout Texas.

★ KELLI NOTO ★

Numbers have never been my forte. My first assignment in kindergarten was to memorize my phone number. My parents practiced with me at dinner and again on the walk to school. A month passed and I still couldn't recite my phone number. My dad sympathized with my frustration. He wrote the numbers on my shoe so I'd be able to peek right before reciting. When I saw the teacher, I looked at my shoe and mumbled the numbers. It felt great to have that task behind me, but even better that my dad cared enough to offer me a way out. I know my phone number now as well as my dad's phone number. Just don't ask me what my cell number is!

⭐ **BARB PFEFFER** ⭐ One of my most memorable school moments occurred during the School Carnival held my kindergarten year. A variety of "white elephant" prizes had been donated by the parents. After winning a game, I selected a beautiful crystal ashtray to give to my mother. When I presented it to her, she started laughing. It turned out that she had been the one to donate the "beautiful" crystal ashtray prize! To this day, our family still laughs about that story.

⭐ **SUZY PLANTAMURA** ⭐ In first grade, I got in so much trouble from my teacher, Mr. Harold. We had a metal cabinet that he used to keep the colored paper in. I loved to organize the drawers, sorting all the colors. One day I asked him over and over if I could clean out the paper drawers and he blew up at me for bugging him. He sent me home early and I can still remember walking home crying.

⭐ **HEATHER PRECKEL** ⭐ I really loved school! My best memories are simply about some of the teachers I had. My favorite teacher was Mrs. Drinkwine, my second grade teacher. (I thought her name was cool!) I just remember really loving her and second grade a lot. To be able to remember her name after all these years makes me realize just how much I looked up to her at that time in my little life!

⭐ **KATHLEEN SUMMERS** ⭐ I remember starting my senior year of high school. I had a great group of friends and a secure relationship with the boy I'd been dating since my junior year. My class load was light and I was happy about being "The Class of '87," the next class to graduate. I still remember some of the fun things we did to kick off the year. And it was indeed a wonderful time...my most favorite of all my school years.

⭐ **CHRISTINE TRAVERSA** ⭐ This photo reminds me of a carefree time in my life, a time when living was easy and free, when life was full of humor. I remember wearing this cheerleading outfit at my grade school, while cheerleading on the sidelines during a basketball game. At one of the games, I did the splits and was hit in the head with two basketballs. I remember laughing really hard with my friends about that experience.

⭐ **DENISE TUCKER** ⭐ I remember fondly the fact that my first grade teacher loved me. Actually, she treasured me more than any of her other students. The reason for that bias was the fact that she was also my mother. I was privileged to have not only the most dedicated and talented first grade teacher on earth, but even more blessed to be able to call her Mom.

★ SOURCE GUIDE ★

The following companies manufacture products featured in this book. Please check your local retailers to find these materials, or go to a company's Web site for the latest product. In addition, we have made every attempt to properly credit the items mentioned in this book. We apologize to any company that we have listed incorrectly, and we would appreciate hearing from you.

7 Gypsies
(877) 749-7797
www.sevengypsies.com

A2Z Essentials
(419) 663-2869
www.a2zessentials.com

ACME Laboratories
www.acme.com

Adobe Systems Incorporated
(866) 766-2256
www.adobe.com

Adorn It / Carolee's Creations
(435) 563-1100
www.adornit.com

American Crafts
(801) 226-0747
www.americancrafts.com

Arctic Frog
(479) 636-FROG
www.arcticfrog.com

Around The Block
(801) 593-1946
www.aroundtheblockproducts.com

Autumn Leaves
(800) 588-6707
www.autumnleaves.com

Avery Dennison Corporation
(800) GO-AVERY
www.avery.com

BasicGrey
(801) 451-6006
www.basicgrey.com

Bazzill Basics Paper
(480) 558-8557
www.bazzillbasics.com

Berwick Offray, LLC
(800) 344-5533
www.offray.com

Bobarbo
(418) 748-6775
www.bobarbo.com

Bo-Bunny Press
(801) 771-4010
www.bobunny.com

Boxer Scrapbook Productions, LLC
(888) 625-6255
www.boxerscrapbooks.com

Carolee's Creations - see Adorn It

ChartPak
(800) 628-1910
www.chartpak.com

Chatterbox, Inc.
(208) 939-9133
www.chatterboxinc.com

Cherry Arte
(212) 465-3495
www.cherryarte.com

Clearsnap, Inc.
(360) 293-6634
www.clearsnap.com

Cloud 9 Design
(763) 493-0990
www.cloud9design.biz

Colorbök, Inc.
(800) 366-4660
www.colorbok.com

Coordinates Collections
(949)370-9865
www.coordinatescollections.com

Craf-T Products
(507) 235-3996
www.craf-tproducts.com

Crate Paper
(702) 966-0409
www.cratepaper.com

Creative Co-op.
(866) 323-2264
www.creativecoop.com

Creative Imaginations
(800) 942-6487
www.cigift.com

Creative Impressions Rubber Stamps, Inc.
(719) 596-4860
www.creativeimpressions.com

Crescent Cardboard Company, LLC
(800) 323-1055
www.crescentcardboard.com

Crossed Paths
(972) 393-3755
www.crossedpaths.net

Dafont
www.dafont.com

Daisy D's Paper Company
(888) 601-8955
www.daisydspaper.com

DDDesigns 7
www.dddesigns7.com

Dèjá Views
(800) 243-8419
www.dejaviews.com

Design Originals
(800) 877-0067
www.d-originals.com

Designer's Library by Lana, The
www.thedesignerslibrary.com

Die Cuts With A View
(801) 224-6766
www.diecutswithaview.com

DMC Corp.
(973) 589-0606
www.dmc.com

Doodlebug Design Inc.
(801) 966-9952
www.doodlebug.ws

Dress It Up
www.dressitup.com

Dymo
(800) 426-7827
www.dymo.com

EK Success, Ltd.
(800) 524-1349
www.eksuccess.com

Everlasting Keepsakes by faith
(816) 896-7037
www.everlastinkeepsakes.com

Family Treasures
(949) 290-0872
www.familytreasures.com

Fancy Pants Designs, LLC
(801) 779-3212
www.fancypantsdesigns.com

Fiskars, Inc.
(800) 950-0203
www.fiskars.com

Flair Designs
(888) 546-9990
www.flairdesignsinc.com

FontWerks
(604) 942-3105
www.fontwerks.com

Frances Meyer, Inc.
(413) 584-5446
www.francesmeyer.com

Freckle Press - no source available

Fredrix Artist Canvas
www.fredrixartistcanvas.com

Gone Scrappin'
(435) 647-0404
www.gonescrappin.com

Grafix
(800) 447-2349
www.grafix.com

Heidi Grace Designs, Inc.
(608) 294-4509
www.heidigrace.com

Heidi Swapp/Advantus Corporation
(904) 482-0092
www.heidiswapp.com

Hero Arts Rubber Stamps, Inc.
(800) 822-4376
www.heroarts.com

Imagination Project, Inc.
(513) 860-2711
www.imaginationproject.com

JewelCraft, LLC
(201) 223-0804
www.jewelcraft.biz

Jolee's Boutique
www.scrapbook.com/jolees

Junkitz
(732) 792-1108
www.junkitz.com

K & Company
(888) 244 2083
www.kandcompany.com

Karen Foster Design
(801) 451-9779
www.karenfosterdesign.com

KI Memories
(972) 243-5595
www.kimemories.com

Kolo, LLC
(888) 636-5656
www.kolo.com

Krylon
(216) 566-200
www.krylon.com

Lettering Delights
www.letteringdelights.com

Li'l Davis Designs
(949) 838-0344
www.lildavisdesigns.com

LumaPix
(877) 506-2740
www.lumapix.com

Magic Mesh
(651) 345 6374
www.magicmesh.com

Magistical Memories
(818) 842-1540
www.magisticalmemories.com

Making Memories
(800) 286-5263
www.makingmemories.com

Mara-Mi, Inc.
(800) 627-2648
www.mara-mi.com

Marvy Uchida/ Uchida of America, Corp.
(800) 541-5877
www.uchida.com

Ma Vinci's Reliquary - no source available

May Arts
(800) 442-3950
www.mayarts.com

Maya Road, LLC
(214) 488-3279
www.mayaroad.com

me & my BiG ideas
(949) 883-2065
www.meandmybigideas.com

Memories Complete, LLC
(866) 966-6365
www.memoriescomplete.com

Michael Miller Memories
(212) 704-0774
www.michaelmillermemories.com

Michaels Arts & Crafts
(800) 642-4235
www.michaels.com

Microsoft Corporation
www.microsoft.com

Mrs. Grossman's Paper Company
(800) 429-4549
www.mrsgrossmans.com

My Mind's Eye, Inc.
(800) 665-5116
www.mymindseye.com

Offray- see Berwick Offray, LLC

Paper Adventures
(973) 406-5000
www.paperadventures.com

Paper Loft
(866) 254-1961
www.paperloft.com

Paper Salon
(952) 445-6878
www.papersalon.com

Paper Studio
(480) 557-5700
www.paperstudio.com

Pebbles Inc.
(801) 224-1857
www.pebblesinc.com

Penny Black, Inc.
www.pennyblackinc.com

Plaid Enterprises, Inc.
(800) 842 4197
www.plaidonline.com

Pressed Petals
(800) 748-4656
www.pressedpetals.com

Prima Marketing, Inc.
(909) 627-5532
www.primamarketinginc.com

Prism Papers
(866) 902-1002
www.prismpapers.com

Provo Craft
(888) 577-3545
www.provocraft.com

PSX Design
(800) 782-6748
www.psxdesign.com

Queen & Co.
(858) 485-5132
www.queenandcompany.com

QuicKutz, Inc.
(801) 765-1144
www.quickutz.com

Ranger Industries, Inc.
(800) 244-2211
www.rangerink.com

Ribbon Girls
www.ribbongirls.net

Ribbon Smyth
(215) 249-9096
www.ribbonsmyth.com

Rusty Pickle
(801) 746-1045
www.rustypickle.com

Scenic Route Paper Co.
(801) 785-0761
www.scenicroutepaper.com

Scrap Pagerz
(435) 645-0696
www.scrappagerz.com

Scrap Therapy Designs, Inc.
(800) 333-7880
www.scraptherapy.com

Scrap Village
www.scrapvillage.com

Scrapworks, LLC
(801) 363-1010
www.scrapworks.com

SEI, Inc.
(800) 333-3279
www.shopsei.com

Shoe Talkers
www.shoetalkers.com

Sizzix
(866) 742-4447
www.sizzix.com

Staples, Inc.
(800) 3STAPLE
www.staples.com

Sticker Studio
(208) 322-2465
www.stickerstudio.com

Sugarloaf Products, Inc.
(770) 484-0722
www.sugarloafproducts.com

Sweetwater
(800) 359-3094
www.sweetwaterscrapbook.com

Target
www.target.com

Technique Tuesday, LLC
(503) 644-4073
www.techniquetuesday.com

Therm O Web, Inc.
(800) 323-0799
www.thermoweb.com

Three Bugs in a Rug
(801) 804-6657
www.threebugsinarug.com

Tri Coastal Design
(80)) 278-9218
www.tricoastaldesigns.com

Tsukineko, Inc.
(800) 769-6633
www.tsukineko.com

Two Peas in a Bucket
(888) 896-7327
www.twopeasinabucket.com

Urban Lily
61-3-9778-5327
www.urbanlily.com

Wal-Mart Stores, Inc.
(800) WALMART
www.walmart.com

We R Memory Keepers, Inc.
(801) 539-5000
www.weronthenet.com

Westrim Crafts
(800) 727-2727
www.westrimcrafts.com

Wordsworth
(719) 282-3495
www.wordsworthstamps.com

Wrights Ribbon Accents
(877) 597-4448
www.wrights.com

Yaley Enterprises
(800) 959-2539
www.yaley.com

Zsiage, LLC
(718) 224-1976
www.zsiage.com

★ INDEX ★

★ A ★

Accomplishments 32-35, 60-63, 88-91, 116-119

Activities 26-31, 52-59, 80-87, 108-115

Altered CD/record, how to 84

Altered paperclip, how to 98

Art activities, school 20, 29, 45, 52, 103, 105

★ B ★

Back to school 10-17, 38-43, 66-71, 94-99

    Jitters 11, 16, 17, 42, 71

    Shopping 41, 69, 94, 97

★ C ★

CD/record, altered, how to 84

★ D ★

Daily routine 18-25, 44-51, 72-79, 100-107

Driving 103, 110

★ E ★

Events

    Crazy hair day 22, 56

    Day, 100th 31

    Field day 57

    Grandparents' day 58

    Picnics 27, 80

    Plays 26, 54

    School dances 84, 87, 112, 113, 114

    Show-n-tell week 30

    Stop, drop & read days 18

★ F ★

Field trips 28, 59, 86

Folder tabs, how to 28

Freshman year 92-119

Friends 15, 40, 48, 51, 72

★ G ★

Gifts for teachers 31

Grade one 8-35

Grade two 36-63

Grade three 36-63

Grade four 36-63

Grade five 36-63

Grade six 64-91

Grade seven 64-91

Grade eight 64-91

Grade nine 92-119

Grade ten 92-119

Grade eleven 92-119

Grade twelve 92-119

Graduation 32, 33, 62, 109, 111, 119

Growth 13, 49, 60, 91, 118

★ H ★

Holidays 29, 34

Home schooling 68, 88, 107

Homework 45, 46, 51, 72, 77

★ J ★

Journaling, ideas for 69

    Fun with words 25

    Interview questions 85

Junior year 92-119

★ K ★

Kids, scrapbooking with 38

Kindergarten 8-35

★ M ★

Memorabilia checklists 10, 95, 111

Mini albums, ideas for 63

Multi photo layout 13, 22, 23, 106, 107, 111, 117

Music 44, 53, 81

★ O ★

Outstanding student 21, 27, 58, 76, 85, 87, 89, 90, 109, 116

★ P ★

Paperclip, altered, how to 98

Photo checklist 18, 57, 80, 105

Picnics, class 27, 80

Plays 26, 54

Preschool 8-35

Prom 112, 113, 114

★ R ★

Reading 18, 19

Routines. *See* Daily routines

★ S ★

School dances 84, 87. *See also* Prom

Senior year

Sophomore year 92-119

Sports 22, 53, 83, 108, 115

Stamped resist, how to 54

★ T ★

Teachers 25, 32

Techniques

    Altered CD 84

    Altered paperclip 98

    Folder tabs 28

    Stamped resist 54

    Transparency 115

    Wax embellishment 21

Transitioning to new school 10, 61, 99

Transparency, how to 115

★ W ★

Wardrobe 75, 95, 96, 98, 101

Wax embellishment, how to 21

★ LEARN MORE FROM THESE INSPIRING TITLES ★
[from Memory Makers Books]

Discover a colossal gallery of never-before-published, contemporary artwork sure to inspire any crafter seeking to capture precious memories and everyday moments in their scrapbooks. Includes CD-Rom with bonus pages and 75 of the best page layout sketches.

Z0349 ★ $24.99 ★ (CAN $32.99)
ISBN-13: 978-1-892127-91-4 ★ ISBN-10: 1-892127-91-1

Learn how to record the life and times of your teen with emotion, feeling and flair. You'll find hundreds of original page ideas including milestones and special events, school honors, sporting events, first jobs, graduation and more.

33489 ★ $19.99 ★ (CAN $27.99)
ISBN-13: 978-1-892127-74-7 ★ ISBN-10: 1-892127-74-1

Learn the proper preservation techniques to ensure your memorabilia is ready for the archival protective environment of scrapbook albums. Discover how to include memorabilia as backgrounds or embellishments or feature it in easy-to-make pockets, pouches, envelopes, enclosures, shakers, frames and more.

Z0011 ★ $19.99 ★ (CAN $26.99)
ISBN-13: 978-1-892127-76-1 ★ ISBN-10: 1-892127-76-8

This exciting book features a unique gathering of scrapbook pages that capture the glorious "live, laugh, love and learn" moments in a child's life. With pages for every skill level and taste, you'll find amazing page ideas for scrapbooking kids ages 5-12.

33440 ★ $19.99 ★ (CAN $27.99)
ISBN-13: 978-1-892127-63-1 ★ ISBN-10: 1-892127-63-6